REALIZING OUR EMPA
Connected to Krishna

HIS HOLINESS
BIR KRISHNA DAS GOSWAMI

Readers interested in the subject matter of this book are invited by ISKCON of North Carolina to correspond with its secretary.

Bir Krishna das Goswami
1032 Dimmocks Mill Road
Hillsborough, North Carolina 27278

Web: bkgoswami.com
Email: bkgoswami@earthlink.net
Facebook: bkgoswami das

Realizing Our Empathic Nature
(English)

THE COVER: In *The Nectar of Devotion*, Chapter 22, it asserts, "[…] because Krsna is the Supreme Personality of Godhead, it is very difficult to approach Him. But the devotees, taking advantage of His compassionate nature, which is represented by Radharani, always pray to Radharani for Krsna's compassion." Radharani is supremely merciful, and we offer our humble obeisances to her lotus feet.

Cover design: Elaine Lanze

*This book is dedicated to
my eternal guide, well-wisher, and spiritual master
His Divine Grace A.C. Bhaktivedanta Swami Prabhupada
an unlimited ocean of compassion who descended to this world
to manifest the compassion of the Supreme Lord.
by delivering the souls of this fallen age to the spiritual realm.*

*His Divine Grace A.C. Bhaktivedanta Swami Prabhupada
Founder Acarya International Society for Krishna Consciousness*

Contents

FOREWORD

When I first joined the Krishna consciousness movement in 1971, my primary focus was to get out of this material world and live in the spiritual world without any further birth, death, disease and old age. Since those days my desires have thankfully matured. Now, my main goal is to please Srila Prabhupada through increasing the number of Krishna conscious people, and facilitating the deepening of relationships between devotees so that we can interact in a true loving way rather than in terms of our roles in society or the rituals that we follow. I pray to Krishna and Prabhupada to raise my level of compassion so that I will be able to accomplish this goal. Generally speaking, I have noticed in my interactions with devotees that we lack a sense of depth in our relationships, which are often characterized by stereotypical language (lingo). This often leads to heavy conflicts rather than to loving relationships between devotees.

Srila Prabhupada states in *The Nectar of Instruction* that our movement progresses because of loving relationships. Thus, if we are unable to deepen our relationships and find difficulty in expressing our feelings and needs, it is not likely that the society of devotees will increase in a real way – and I am not just speaking about numbers of devotees or numbers of temples being constructed. As I said in my *vyasa puja* offering to Srila Prabhupada, my prayers and my meditation on Radha and Krishna have focused on developing true love and compassion for all of Krishna's parts and parcels. Every desire tree that I approach during my visits to Vrindavana and other holy places hear this supplication from me. This *sankalpa* (intention, desire) is inseparable from my desire to please Srila Prabhupada. I am certain that he will be pleased if I can bring deeply committed souls to his lotus feet. In order to accomplish this I must be able to reflect Prabhupada's compassion, which is what drew me to the Krishna consciousness movement.

I have come to the realization that merely praying for compassion is not enough. One must consciously practice it. Whenever I perceive someone opposing me or showing negativity towards me or my actions, I make that person a special object of my compassion. I pray intensely for him or her. This helps me develop the Vaisnava quality of *ajata satrava* (not having enemies but being everyone's well-wisher). Prahlada Maharaja rejected the concept of friends and enemies that his teachers tried to force on him.

Instead, he regarded all living entities equally (*yas tu sarvani . . . Sri Isopanisad*). In fact, although his father attempted to kill him, Prahlad made him the special object of his compassion. His quality of forgiveness and love for all living entities deeply inspires me.

As a result of the prayer and practice I mentioned, and of course through the mercy of Srila Prabhupada and Radha Govinda, I feel a radical softening of the heart and love for Krishna's parts and parcels. The process actually works! Such intense love for Krishna and his parts and parcels yields the greatest of happiness. Sometimes when I see people, I become overwhelmed by love for them, and I desire to help them become happy in Krishna consciousness. I don't know whether it is good to reveal my mind and heart in this way, but I feel compelled to do it in the hope of inspiring others in their development of Krishna consciousness. Spiritual advancement is not something that is very difficult to attain. It is merely a matter of following the process, but that following should not be done in an external way. It has to truly engage one's heart and soul. Srila Prabhupada has given us the greatest gift, and if we dedicate our lives to passing the gift on to others, success will be quickly attained. These feelings inspire me to look for ways to bring more people to Krishna consciousness; they have awakened my creative impulses to try some innovative ways of sharing Krishna consciousness with others.

The desire for feeling and practicing compassion has led me to take the practical action of studying sociology and relationship strategies with the aim of helping the devotees develop a functional "love-giving" society. I feel pain when I don't see devotees experiencing great happiness. So, I naturally want to facilitate their attainment of blissful Krishna consciousness. I can see that there are many interpersonal and communication issues with which devotees are struggling. I have heard people comment that, even though our movement has the most personal philosophy, we often act rather impersonally – more impersonally it seems, than the impersonalists we decry. Having seen this myself and having talked about it with many devotees, I began investigating methods of conflict resolution. There are methodologies to resolve conflict, but most of them deal exclusively with the specific conflicts at hand rather than the deepening of relationships. Therefore, I searched for something that would transform devotees' consciousness with respect to relationships, both internally and externally, and facilitate the development of loving exchanges between Vaisnavas. It should also naturally support the process of giving and accepting gifts, revealing one's mind in confidence, listening to others, helping others and being empathic with each other.

There are two ways of being compassionate (empathic). The first is by sharing our needs with others – being vulnerable! One can only be vulnerable if one has emotional independence, or emotional freedom (see chapter three). The second is by empathic listening, or receiving empathically from others. Empathy means to be completely in contact, completely aware, and completely caring. It is the art of caring about other people's needs.

My search for understanding brought me to the teachings of *Nonviolent Communication* (NVC) by Marshal B. Rosenberg, PhD., which deals with an individual's underlying basic needs, and formulates practical working strategies for fulfilling all these needs in a win-win fashion – those of others, as well as our own needs. I studied NVC, attended workshops, and, in order to make what I learned useful for devotees, I adapted the NVC principles of need facilitation to Krishna consciousness. In the process, I developed workshops and seminars that have been well-received in the society of devotees.

Empathy in the context of these workshops is defined as listening to and connecting with others, and ourselves, with great compassion and without judgment.

It's crucial to be cautious regarding the habitual use of divisive, judgmental language. The *sastras* contain very clear descriptions, as it is necessary to present the *siddhanta* in a way that does not result in confusion; yet, one should be cautious in applying these designations in everyday life if one wants to develop empathic relationships.

Throughout my years in ISKCON, I have observed the devotees facing many interpersonal and intrapersonal challenges in connection with external and/or internal conflicts. Conflicts, are a natural part of life and neither can, nor should be sidestepped. The challenge is to resolve these conflicts. Compassion (empathy) is the greatest tool for resolving them. It is not a tool for management but for changing one's consciousness in order to connect with others empathically, resolve conflicts in a win-win way, and ultimately empower compassionate devotees to form strong cooperative communities. The purpose of this book is to present the basic skills and knowledge needed for practicing empathic communication and allowing it to become a transformative agent in our lives.

ACKNOWLEDGEMENTS

I first want to acknowledge Marshall Rosenberg, his book, "Non Violent Communication, the Language for Life" and all his seminars and practice groups that have brought us to a deeper understanding of how to communicate compassionately. The methodology is adapted and from the principles outlined in his book.

I would like to thank the following devotees who helped me in different ways such as transcribing, proofreading, editing, and giving feedback to put this book together. It has been a labor of love that has taken many years.

Dukhahantri devi dasi, Gopi devi dasi, Elaine Lanze, Sukhavaha devi dasi, Manjari Gopi devi dasi, Jaya Gauranga das, and Syama Sakhi devi dasi

INTRODUCTION

Srila Bhaktivinoda Thakura mentions that we have material as well as spiritual needs, and to progress smoothly on the spiritual path, both types of needs should be addressed. With this understanding in mind I tried to understand why many devotees have problems in their spiritual lives and relationships. I found the teachings of Marshall B. Rosenberg, the author of the book "*Nonviolent Communication: A Language of Life*" to be helpful in understanding this challenge (and how to deal with it) in light of Bhaktivinoda Thakura's precepts. The result was *Empathic Communication*.

I use the term empathic, because it means having compassion for others which is the hallmark of an evolved devotee. My interest lies in transforming relationships so that the devotees in a Krishna conscious society can live functional lives, materially as well as spiritually. In this book, you will find recommendations which you can utilize to help you develop compassion and empathy in conjunction with the process of Krishna Consciousness, as given to us by His Divine Grace Srila Prabhupada. When I say process, I don't mean some merely mechanical process. Although, initially, there are some mechanics, it is actually a question of changing the heart, being concerned for and wanting to connect with others. It is, thus, not just a language, though we do use language for reshaping our consciousness. If we are not sensitive to the words we use, we can drive people away from, instead of towards, Krishna's lotus feet.

Empathic Communication (EC) can be applied at all levels of communication; intimate relations, families, schools, organizations, therapies, negotiation, conflicts, etc. It's not required that the other person know the EC process or even be motivated to use it. One person is sufficient to start the process of connecting. This can assist us in bringing situations to resolution and help to free ourselves from the obstructive effects of past experiences and conditioning. Empathic communication allows us to break the pattern of thinking that is at the foundation of arguments, anger, and depression, to resolve conflicts peacefully and build relationships on mutual respect, compassion, and cooperation.

One should know the difference between real compassion (whether transcendental or material) and sheer sentimentalism or sympathy (see chapter one). This difference between empathy and sympathy will be explained in the first chapter. If we comprehend this difference, we will be able to discern *true* compassion from *sentimental* sympathy. Therefore, the focus of the first chapter is about compassion. The second chapter explores how the structures of society contribute to disconnection and violence, how we use power in various relationships, and how we block compassion in communication. The third chapter covers in depth, the complete process of Empathic Communication as well as how to develop strategies that can be practically used in empathic communication, from connecting to ourselves and others to dealing with anger. The fourth chapter is about raising children empathically in Krishna consciousness, and the fifth chapter deals with the expression of heartfelt gratitude and appreciation.

CHAPTER ONE

What Is Empathy?

The Difference between Empathy and Sympathy

What is the difference between empathy and sympathy? Common English doesn't actually differentiate between empathy and sympathy. Sometimes empathy is used synonymously with sympathy, but sympathy often carries a negative connotation and a judgmental tone; therefore, I prefer to use empathy. Sympathy is concerned with my feelings towards another. Whereas empathy is concerned with my attempting to understand another's feelings and needs. So, this book designates real or *true* compassion as empathy.

There is a need to distinguish between *true* compassion (whether transcendental or material) and *sentimental* compassion, which can be harmful to living entities. Prabhupada gives the example of a young boy who suffered from liver disease. His brother, feeling sympathetic towards him, gave him fried foods and sweets. Both are very bad for a compromised liver. This exemplifies that without proper understanding, acts motivated by compassion can hurt the living entity. This applies to both the material and spiritual interactions. Compassion (empathy) is in accord with the *sastras*,

When we feel sympathy for someone, the focus is on our emotions connected with their situation. For example, if you tell a person who is suffering from a toothache, "I feel really bad for you," what does this actually do for that person? Not much. Our feeling "bad" for a distressed person helps neither them nor us. Imagine that you are in pain and somebody says that they feel really bad for you. How does that affect you? It doesn't make the pain go away. That's sympathy, because it's not in tune with someone's feelings. It is quite different from Krishna consciousness compassion.

Before I joined the movement, my mother used to engage in various social welfare activities. When I asked her about her acts of charity, she said that it made her feel good. That was sympathy; You choose to do something because it "makes you feel good" or because it would "make you feel guilty" if you didn't do it. The motivation is personal and not connected to the other person's feelings or needs.

Sympathy means that we are thinking about ourselves. It's unfortunate that many therapists even deal with their clients in this way. I once observed a trained social worker counseling a devotee who had been traumatized as a child. The social worker said, "I feel so sad for you." It did not offer any benefit to the person, because sympathy doesn't address or acknowledge an individual's feelings or needs. It's just another instance of talking about oneself. It's important to ask ourselves, "Where is the focus – on *me*, or them?"

In contrast to this there is empathy, which takes the other person's feelings and needs as its focal point. The Sanskrit term for this is *para duhkha duhkhi*, regarding another's feelings as more important than one's own. You help the person much more by being empathic.

How do you get to the point of being *para duhkha duhkhi* instead of just being sympathetic? Let's go back to the example of the toothache. You are really suffering, and someone says in a compassionate and reflective manner, "You must be in a lot of pain because of that toothache. It must be very stressful for you." This is an expression of empathy. For example, if someone is visibly sad, we can personally reflect that emotion by saying, "Are you feeling extremely unhappy today?" This personal reflection can offer comfort. You should also reflect their feelings through the tone of voice, and body language. Empathy starts with the internal intention to connect with another being. It is not about the words but about the personal connection.

Empathy means presence, being there for somebody, being in touch with his or her feelings and at the same time in touch with yourself, with your own feelings and needs. This makes the connection personal and complete, reciprocal. In third chapter of this book I will elaborate on this in practical terms. Empathy – or presence – is focus, wonder, caring and intention. It is caring for people without judgment. Empathy is *not* grilling, analyzing, recommending, counseling, educating, managing or repairing. Focus and care will foster empathic connections.

Some professional therapists say that you have to sit in a certain position and act in a certain way to communicate compassion. In a course I attended, it was stated that, in order to really be empathic with people, you have to lean forward, show interest, and not cross your legs. In my experience, it doesn't work like that, because real empathy is a state of consciousness. If we rely on externalities it becomes artificial and static. Empathy means connecting by being personally (with one's heart and mind) present and fully aware of the other person's feelings and needs. You may sit in any way that allows for this connection to take place.

Obviously, you should not be constantly looking at your watch. Looking at the other person is important, as is awareness of body language and tone of voice – more so than words. In fact, you don't even have to say anything at all. Empathy is expressed by one's consciousness. What is meant to be shared will be shared. Empathy is holistic and is expressed with every aspect of one's being.

Tolerance

To be able to feel and express compassion tolerance is essential. One of the first lessons Krishna gives in the Bhagavad-gita concerns tolerance.

matra-sparsas tu kaunteya   sitosna-sukha-duhkha-dah
agamapayino nityas   tams titiksasva bharata

*"O son of Kunti, the nonpermanent appearance of happiness and distress, and their disappearance in due course are like the appearance and disappearance of the winter and summer seasons. They arise from sense perception, O son of Bharata and one must learn to tolerate them without being disturbed."*1

Tolerance is a preliminary step in the development of compassion. All living beings are part and parcel of Krishna. They are our brothers and sisters. Understanding this, we can make a conscious effort to become humble, tolerant and loving towards others.

In Srimad Bhagavatam, Lord Kapiladeva describes the saintly qualities of a devotee as follows:

titiksavah karunikah
suhrdah sarva-bhutanam

---

1 *Bhagavad Gita 2.14.*

Realizing Our Empathic Nature

ajata-satravah santah
sadhavah sadhu-bhusanah

*"The symptoms of a sadhu are that he is tolerant, merciful, and friendly to all living entities. He has no enemies, he is peaceful, he abides by the scriptures and all his characteristics are sublime."*2

PURPORT: A sadhu, as described above, is a devotee of the Lord. His concern, therefore, is to enlighten people in devotional service to the Lord. That is his mercy. He knows that without devotional service to the Lord, human life is spoiled. A devotee travels all over the country, from door to door preaching, "Be Krsna conscious. Be a devotee of Lord Krsna. Don't spoil your life in simply fulfilling your animal propensities. Human life is meant for self-realization, or Krsna consciousness." These are the preachings of a sadhu. He is not satisfied with his own liberation. He always thinks about others. He is the most compassionate personality towards all the fallen souls. One of his qualifications, therefore, is *karunika*, great mercy to the fallen souls. While engaged in preaching work, he has to meet with so many opposing elements, and therefore the sadhu, or devotee of the Lord, has to be very tolerant. Someone may ill-treat him because the conditioned souls are not prepared to receive the transcendental knowledge of devotional service. They do not like it; that is their disease. The sadhu has the thankless task of impressing upon them the importance of devotional service. Sometimes devotees are personally attacked with violence. Lord Jesus Christ was crucified, Haridasa Thakura was caned in twenty-two marketplaces, and Lord Caitanya's principal assistant, Nityananda, was violently attacked by Jagai and Madhai. But still they were tolerant because their mission was to deliver the fallen souls. One of the qualifications of a sadhu is that he is very tolerant and is merciful to all fallen souls. He is merciful because he is the well-wisher of all living entities.3

---

2 *Srimad Bhagavatam 3.25.21*

3 *Ibid.*

It's important to learn how to tolerate and avoid thinking that those who satisfy my senses are friends, and those who do not satisfy my senses are enemies. When we think in terms of friends and enemies, only certain people will be objects of our empathy and others will not, simply because they don't please our senses. That is not Krishna consciousness, but self centeredness. Prahlad Maharaja's teachers were attempting to teach him this concept of friends and enemies. He rejected these distinctions as being demoniac. Unfortunately, most of us have not rejected this dichotomy yet.

There are, however, specific situations where it is not appropriate to tolerate certain behavoir. For example, one should not tolerate blasphemy of Krishna or His devotee or physical violence. That intolerance is actually spiritual, because it's out of love, rather than frustrated lust. If we hear someone say, "Krishna originates in the Brahman," or "He's impersonal," it generates anger; because one loves Krishna. And you can express that anger, but properly, philosophically. That type of anger arises from love for Krishna. It is not frustration, it is love.

How Can We Develop Tolerance?

We can develop tolerance by acting in a way that is pleasing to Krishna. If we act out of love for Krishna, we'll be ready to tolerate for His sake. A story that illustrates how one can develop tolerance is the story of Dharma the bull. He was being beaten by Kali, and was standing on one leg, urinating. When Maharaja Pariksit came, and asked him, "Who did this to you?!" Dharma the bull did not reply: "Kali did it! Get him! Let me see him suffer now!" He answered instead, "It is very difficult to ascertain." He saw the Lord behind these difficult circumstances. Dharma the bull said that anyone blaming the immediate perpetrator, who appears to be the cause, becomes just as culpable as the immediate perpetrator. If Dharma the bull had said to Pariksit Maharaja, "Kali is at fault. He caused my pain," he would have become as culpable as Kali. Similarly, it's invaluable as practicing devotees to tolerate everything that happens to us, good or bad, and see it as the result of our past activities given to us for our purification. There is a nice verse in Srimad Bhagavatam spoken by Lord Brahma that teaches us how to become tolerant.

tat te 'nukampah susamiksamano
bhunjana evatma-krtam vipakam

Realizing Our Empathic Nature

hrd-vag-vapurbhir vidadhan namas te
jiveta yo mukti-pade sa daya-bhak

"My dear Lord, one who earnestly waits for You to bestow Your causeless mercy upon him, all the while patiently suffering the reactions of his past misdeeds and offering You respectful obeisances with his heart, words and body, is surely eligible for liberation, for it has become his rightful claim."[4]

Sometimes it is easier to tolerate difficult situations rather than pleasant ones, as pleasant ones have the ability to bewilder us more than challenging ones. It is essential as devotees to see Krishna behind everything. For a devotee, every situation is directly administered by Krishna. If someone has not yet taken up Krishna consciousness, then it is a reaction directed by the laws of Karma. For one on the path of spiritual advancement, it is Krishna and He is doing it to teach us a specific lesson. Krishna says in the Bhagavad-gita,

yo mam pasyati sarvatra   sarvam ca mayi pasyati
tasyaham na pranasyami   sa ca me na pranasyati

"For one who sees Me everywhere and sees everything in Me, I am never lost, nor is he ever
lost to Me."[5]

If one sees like this, then he understands that whatever happens is for his own benefit. It is Krishna's arrangement. Srila Prabhupada, too, states, *"Not a blade of grass moves without the will of the Supreme Personality of Godhead."* [6] Developing this frame of mind can help us develop tolerance, which is the prerequisite for compassion.

These qualities, tolerance and compassion, were perfectly demonstrated by Prabhupada. One of the reasons for Srila Prabhupada's success is that he was truly tolerant. Can you imagine the degree of tolerance he had? In Vrindavana he was at home surrounded by Vaisnavas, but in America he

---

4 *Srimad Bhagavatam* 10.14.8.

5 *Bhagavad-gita 6.30.*

6 *Bhagavad-gita 7.21., purport*

was living with people who were unclean and engaged in abominable activities. His God brothers criticized him. Without understanding, they said, "Oh, he was successful because he liked to hang out with the Westerners." But Srila Prabhupada was so successful because as a *nitya siddha* (pure devotee) Mahabhagavata he was immersed in love for Krishna and all Krishna's parts and parcels (the living entities). Prabhupada loved us as a mother loves her children.

Srila Bhaktisiddhanta Sarasvati Thakur illustrated the necessity of tolerance. He said in order to make devotees we have to shed gallons of blood. He said too, "If they want meat, feed them meat, but give them Krishna consciousness." It's not that we should actually distribute meat. This was a demonstration of his tolerance, an example that we don't follow literally. His mood was to do whatever is necessary to bring people to Krishna consciousness and to tolerate their bad habits along the way. Srila Prabhupada also exhibited this topmost aspect, this topmost manifestation of empathy and tolerance.

Within our scriptures, we find numerous examples of great tolerant personalities. One of my favorites is Prahlad Maharaja. Prahlad did not pray for the Lord to kill His father. During the time that he was being tormented he never asked Lord Nrisimhadeva to smash his father.

Sometimes people become joyful to see someone else suffer. If someone commits the crime of murder and consequently gets put to death by lethal injection or the electric chair in America we see that outside of the prison, there is an event going on that is called 'tailgating.' People gather together, sit in their pickup trucks drinking beer and wait for the person's execution to take place. As soon as news gets out that the condemned man is dead, they jump up and start shouting, "This is great! Now he's dead!" Of course, we understand that in some instances capital punishment is necessary for the good of the person being punished and for society. However, it should not be enacted with the mood of retribution.

Prahlad Maharaja was not like this. The whole time that his father was torturing him, Prahlad just chanted the Holy Names of Krishna. He felt no animosity towards his father and never got angry with anyone that was attacking him. He never considered them to be his enemies, nor did he ever pray for his own bodily protection. His prayers were for attaining pure devotional service as well as for the welfare of those who tormented him. When the Lord destroyed Hiranyakasipu, Prahlad did not say, "I'm glad that my father was killed. Let him suffer!" Instead, he asked of Lord Nrsimhadeva, "Please save him!"

After his ordeal, he exhibited compassion for all of the fallen conditioned souls. Even when the Lord offered him anything, Prahlad first declined, stating that he was not a merchant (someone who was doing service in exchange for something in return). Finally, he did ask for something, although not for himself. Prahlad was so overwhelmed with empathy for the conditioned souls, especially his father, that he begged the Lord to give them His mercy. I regard Prahlad as the perfect example of Vaisnava tolerance, love, mercy and purity. He is a shining source of inspiration for me in my spiritual life.

Compassion

The word compassion means "feeling together with." Com–passion: passion means feeling, and doesn't always refer to the *mode of passion*. In this particular context, it means "with feeling." Compassion thus means "feeling with others." To be clear, compassion is not an inert emotion as in, "I feel sorry for you." Nor is it theoretical knowledge or calculations. It is a *bhava*. It is an emotion that pulls you to act in a certain way. Compassionate people forget about their own self-interest and help others. This is a very exalted platform. Yet, we can start to practice it at our level of advancement by making the effort to understand its meaning, then acting upon that understanding. Prabhupada told us action in knowledge yields realization.

"A person who is unable to bear another's distress is called compassionate,"[7] as declared in *The Nectar of Devotion*. Compassion and love for all living entities are the hallmark of Krishna consciousness.

The greatest suffering is to be ignorant of one's original position as Krishna's servant. Living entities have been wandering in this material world since time immemorial. Only a devotee's mercy can free them. But, if this mercy is not transmitted in a compassionate manner, people will not be willing to accept it. They will see the devotees as judging them and wanting to forcibly change their lives. It is useful for devotees to acquire proper communication skills in order to share Krishna Consciousness in a balanced way, and also be with Vaisnavas without hurting or offending them. An ideal Vaiṣṇava society is based on the principle of compassion. What is presented in this book is not mere theoretical knowledge or an analysis of a spiritual topic, but something essential to be applied in practice.

> ". . . But no one knows where compassion should be applied. Compassion for the dress of a drowning man is senseless. A man fallen in the ocean of nescience cannot be saved simply by rescuing his outward dress—the gross material body."[8]

7*The Nectar of Devotion,* chapter 22, page 175.

8 *Bhagavad Gita 2.1*

It is vital for us to be very clear about our priorities, and our first priority is being Krishna conscious ourselves and giving Krishna consciousness to others. That is how devotees show their spiritual compassion for the fallen souls. Various misconceptions may prevail among devotees. Devotees may think that we are not concerned about the material suffering of people, such as diseases, starvation, poverty, natural disasters, wars and so forth. They assume that giving Krishna consciousness to others is not only the most important, but also the *exclusive* welfare activity, and therefore there is no need to be involved in any other work. Our main concern is distributing transcendental knowledge to others, but when we have the opportunity to assist people personally, it is important to show our compassion for their material sufferings. As humans, we have the capacity to understand the pain felt by others.

Devotees are happy to distribute *prasadam* to hungry people or to assist someone old or sick by rendering simple acts of kindness. When we see beggars, we give them some prasadam or a few small coins. Srila Bhaktisiddhanta Sarasvati Thakura corrected his disciples for being uncharitable to the beggars in Vrindavana because their refusal to give something evidenced their false pride thinking of themselves as great devotees. He told them, "*If you do not give alms, thinking you are better than the beggars since you are a devotee, it will make you hardhearted.*" Srimad Bhagavatam relates this as follows:

> "*Therefore, all the great sages assembled together and after observing cruel Vena's atrocities concluded that a great danger and catastrophe was approaching the people of the world. Thus, out of compassion they began to talk amongst themselves, for they themselves were the performers of the sacrifices.*"[9]

PURPORT: Before King Vena was enthroned, all the great sages were very much anxious to see to the welfare of society. When they saw that King Vena was most irresponsible, cruel and atrocious, they again began to think of the welfare of the people. It should be understood that sages, saintly persons and devotees are not unconcerned with the people's welfare. Ordinary karmis are busy acquiring money for sense gratification, and ordinary jnanis

---

9*Srimad-Bhagavatam*, 4.14.7 and *Srimad-Bhagavatam*, 4.14.7 purport

are socially aloof when they speculate on liberation, but actual devotees and saintly persons are always anxious to see how the people can be made happy both materially and spiritually. Therefore, the great sages began to consult one another on how to get out of the dangerous atmosphere created by King Vena.[10]

Concern for others is a symptom of someone who has a soft heart and does not like to see others in pain. A devotee does not like to see any type of suffering whether it is material or spiritual; at the same time, we cannot simply change our priorities and become a humanitarian organization instead of one that spreads *bhakti*. When devotees are mistakenly indifferent to the suffering of others the tendency is to become hardhearted, and risk becoming unconcerned with giving others Krishna consciousness. If both kinds of awareness are there, a devotee is truly compassionate. Empathy will progress parallel with eagerness to give the mercy of the holy name. As Bhaktivinode Thakura says, *"jive doya, krsna-nama-sarva-dharma-sara."*[11] The essence of all forms of religion is compassion toward the living beings and the chanting of Krishna's names.

Compassion will manifest in our hearts when we follow our spiritual master's instructions. Engaging in preaching, book distribution, *harinama*, *prasadam* distribution or any Krishna conscious activity to help others, our hearts will gradually become softer. A pure devotee has a soft heart. If one hears of others' suffering and merely says, "That's life or that's their karma," it is evidence of a hard heart. A softhearted devotee is compelled to do something.

In Mayapur, when Srila Prabhupada saw children fighting with the dogs for the remnants of prasadam, he cried. He immediately gave orders that no one within a certain radius of the temple was to go hungry. That is a soft heart. We too must seek to develop this sense of compassion and empathy for others. It is the essence of what makes one a Vaiṣṇava.

10*Ibid.*

11Srila Bhaktivinoda Thakura, *Gitavali, Nagara Kirtana, 1. song Ajna-tahal*

How Do We Develop a Compassionate Nature?

Developing and manifesting compassion is essential. We cannot separate Krishna consciousness from compassion toward others. We can develop these qualities in a practical way by associating with and serving the Vaishnavas. Theoretically, the first step in developing a compassionate outlook is to understand that all living beings are part and parcel of Krishna, and that He is not satisfied if we direct our love only towards Him. This is confirmed in *Sri Isopanisad*.

yas tu sarvani bhutany
atmany evanupasyati
sarva-bhutesu catmanam
tato na vijugupsate

"He who sees systematically everything in relation to the Supreme Lord, who sees all living entities as His parts and parcels, and who sees the Supreme Lord within everything, never hates anything or any being."[12]

There are many similar verses in the Vedic literature. When we see everyone in relationship to Krishna, then we understand the relationship we have with everyone else, which is a family relationship. This is similar to a mother having an empathic relationship with her child because she is naturally concerned for the child's wellbeing. Srila Prabhupada said that the love that a mother has for a child is the closest thing to pure love that we find in this world. We can learn by watching this interaction because of her *sambandha*, relationship, with the child. The reason we are not able to truly love people is that we don't experience a true *sambandha* with them.

So how can we develop *sambandha*? The very first step is to develop our relationship with Krishna, and we can do that by following the processes of *bhakti-yoga*. Meditating on and remembering the fact that everyone is part and parcel of Krishna will help us see others and ourselves in connection with Krishna. In this way, will we perceive everybody as part of our spiritual family, and we will not fall victim to the mentality that Lord Kapila condemns in the Srimad Bhagavatam.

12*Sri Isopanisad* mantra 6.

aham sarvesu bhutesu
bhutatmavasthitau sada
tam avajnaya mam martyah
kurute 'rca-vidambanam

"One who worships the Deity of Godhead in the temples but does not know that the Supreme Lord, as Paramatma, is situated in every living entity's heart, must be in ignorance and is compared to one who offers oblations into ashes."[13]

Kripa Sindhu: An Ocean of Compassion

Compassion arises from *svarupa sakti*, the internal potency of the Lord. It manifests from the combination of *hladini* and *samvit saktis*. When we are in knowledge (*samvit*) of the suffering of others and possess love for all living entities, then we will be capable of feeling real compassion. As previously mentioned, that compassion or empathy is substantiated by our giving others the treasure of love of Godhead, and by trying to minimize their material suffering and by helping them understand the root cause of their suffering.

Lord Krishna is the original compassionate personality. *The Nectar of Devotion* asserts this: "Krsna's compassion was also exhibited when Grandfather Bhisma was lying on the bed of arrows which had been shot through his body. While lying in this position, Bhisma was very anxious to see Krsna, and thus Krsna appeared there. Upon seeing the pitiable condition of Bhisma, Krsna began speaking with tears in His eyes. Not only was He shedding tears, but He also forgot Himself in His compassion. Therefore, instead of offering obeisances to Krsna directly, devotees offer obeisances to His compassionate nature. Actually, because Krsna is the Supreme Personality of Godhead, it is very difficult to approach Him. But the devotees, taking advantage of His compassionate nature which is represented by Radharani, always pray to Radharani for Krsna's compassion."[14]

13*Srimad Bhagavatam* 3.29.22.

14*The Nectar of Devotion,* chapter 22

We can see thus that the Vaishnavas' compassion is not their own. That ocean of unlimited compassion or mercy primarily resides in Radha-Krishna, and we receive the mercy through the mercy of our spiritual master. *Gurv-astaka* gives the analogy that it is just like clouds pouring water on a forest fire. Although water does not belong to the cloud but comes from the ocean, the cloud is the agent through which water reaches the forest. Since a devotee's compassion or mercy comes from an ocean of mercy, a devotee, too, possesses an ocean of mercy. Ocean stands for "unlimited," We chant every morning "*kripa sindhubhya eva ca.*" The general translation of *kripa-sindhubhya* is "full of compassion." However, the word *sindhu* means more than just full. It means "ocean." Ocean is referred to here because the ocean has an unlimited supply of water. So, "unlimited compassion" would be the better translation. In the same way that an ocean is unlimited, devotees have unlimited compassion for everyone.

Srila Prabhupada's books greatly inspired me in my search for real compassion or empathy, and this verse from Srimad Bhagavatam particularly strikes me in this regard.

yad bhrajamanam sva-rucaiva sarvato
lokas trayo hy anu vibhrajanta ete
yan navrajan jantusu ye 'nanugraha
vrajanti bhadrani caranti ye 'nisam

"The self-effulgent Vaikuntha planets, by whose illumination alone all the illuminating planets within this material world give off reflected light, cannot be reached by those who are not merciful to other living entities. Only persons who constantly engage in welfare activities for other living entities can reach the Vaikuntha planets."15

For me, the operative word in this verse is "constantly." In order to achieve such constancy one has to be compelled by intense love and compassion for all living entities. In real love and compassion there is equality, and hierarchy vanishes like the mist being burnt off by sunshine.

We often compare a Vaiṣṇava to an ocean of compassion (kripa sindhu). It

---

15 *Srimad Bhagavatam 4.12.36.*

is important to understand how this can be, in what way it manifests, and how this ocean is achieved. For example, look at Jayananda Thakura's kripa sindhu, and how Srila Prabhupada showed great compassion and empathy toward him and expressed his appreciation for him. Jayananda Thakura had unlimited compassion for others. Everyone loved him for it. No one in this world hated Jayananda. He served Prabhupada impelled by love. Jayananda Thakura's love for Prabhupada was incomprehensible. He prayed much in the same way as Haridas Thakura had done, that he would not have to witness Prabhupada's final pastimes on this earth, and that he would be allowed to serve Prabhupada eternally. Krishna fulfilled this desire, and Jayananda Thakura got to depart right before his beloved spiritual master.

Letter to Jayananda, May 5, 1977:

My Dear Jayananda,

Please accept my blessings.

I am feeling very intensely your separation. In 1967 you joined me in San Francisco. You were driving my car and chanting Hare Krishna. You were the first man to give me some contribution ($5,000) for printing my Bhagavad-gita. After that, you have rendered very favorable service to Krishna in different ways. I so hope at the time of your death you were remembering Krishna and as such, you have been promoted to the eternal association of Krishna. If not, if you had any tinge of material desire, you have gone to the celestial kingdom to live with the demigods for many thousands of years and enjoy the most opulent life of material existence. From there you can promote yourself to the spiritual world. But even if one fails to promote himself to the spiritual world, at that time he comes down again on the surface of this globe and takes birth in a big family like a yogi's or a brahmana's or an aristocratic family, where there is again chance of reviving Krishna Consciousness. But as you were hearing Krishna-kirtan, I am sure that you were directly promoted to Krishna-loka.

janma karma ca me divyam
evam yo vetti tattvatah
tyaktva deham punar janma
naiti man eti so' rjuna

Krishna has done a great favor to you, not to continue your diseased body, and has given you a suitable place for your service. Thank you very much. Your ever well-wisher,

A.C. Bhaktivedanta Swami

Srila Prabhupada showed the ideal personal example of how Krishna consciousness should be executed. He was completely in touch with his needs and very empathic towards all. His life is a perfect demonstration of spiritual harmony and balance.

> *"The spiritual master is called acarya-vigraha, or the manifestation of the Lord of whom one must take shelter. Only out of His immense compassion does the Personality of Godhead reveal Himself as the spiritual master. Therefore, in the dealings of an acarya there are no activities but those of transcendental loving service to the Lord. He is the Supreme Personality of Godhead's servitor. It is worthwhile to take shelter of such a steady devotee, who is called acarya-vigraha, or the manifestation or form of the Lord of whom one must take shelter."16*

Attaining Self-realization by Showing Compassion

According to the statement of *Srimad Bhagavatam* one becomes a self-realized soul by manifesting the quality of compassion. Srila Prabhupada explains this nicely in his purport to the following verse.

> *kṛtvā dayāṁ ca jīveṣu*
> *dattvā cābhayam ātmavān*
> *mayy ātmānaṁ saha jagad*
> *drakṣyasy ātmani cāpi mām*

> *"Showing compassion to all living entities, you will attain self-realization. Giving assurance of safety to all, you will perceive your own self as well as all the universes in Me, and Myself in you."17*

---

16 *Sri Caitanya-Caritamrta Adi-lila 1.46*

17*Srimad-Bhagavatam*, 3.21.31.

PURPORT: The simple process of self-realization for every living entity is described here. The first principle to be understood is that this world is a product of the supreme will. ... So here also the Lord says, "You will see everything in the world to be nondifferent from Me." This means that everything should be considered a product of the Lord's energy, and therefore everything should be employed in the service of the Lord. One's energy should be utilized for one's self-interest. That is the perfection of the energy.

This energy can be utilized for real self-interest if one is compassionate. A person in Kṛṣṇa consciousness, a devotee of the Lord, is always compassionate. He is not satisfied that only he himself is a devotee, but he tries to distribute the knowledge of devotional service to everyone. There are many devotees of the Lord who faced many risks in distributing the devotional service of the Lord to people in general. That should be done.

It is also said that a person who goes to the temple of the Lord and worships with great devotion, but who does not show sympathy to people in general or show respect to other devotees, is considered to be a third-class devotee. The second-class devotee is he who is merciful and compassionate to the fallen soul. The second-class devotee is always cognizant of his position as an eternal servant of the Lord; he therefore makes friendships with devotees of the Lord, acts compassionately toward the general public in teaching them devotional service, and refuses to cooperate or associate with nondevotees. As long as one is not compassionate to people in general in his devotional service to the Lord, he is a third-class devotee. The first-class devotee gives assurance to every living being that there is no need to fear this material existence. "Let us live in Kṛṣṇa consciousness and conquer the nescience of material existence." It is indicated here that Kardama Muni was directed by the Lord to be very compassionate and liberal in his householder life, and to give assurance to the people in his renounced life.

Because self-realization is the goal of human life, developing a compassionate attitude and behavior is the core of all our spiritual practices. By caring for others, we will give assurance of their safety on all levels. One of our main needs is connection, and for someone to be empathic with us. People often go to astrologers just because they want someone to listen to them and talk about them. People spend money going to a psychologist because of their need for someone to listen to them.

There was once a study done with psychologists who were trained in different methodologies. In this study, they went to a mental institution full of people who were struggling with different issues. The psychologists tried to help the people utilizing their different techniques and the results were studied to determine which theory's representative would be more successful. Some of these psychologists were following Sigmund Freud, some Carl Jung, and some B.F. Skinner. The members of a fourth group were not psychologists at all. They were members of the general public; not trained specialists. It turned out that each of the groups had varying results. The degree of success depended on how much empathy the counselors showed, not on theories, education or academic degrees.

Compassion or empathy is originally present within every human being's heart. It is an innate human quality. Our original spiritual nature is one hundred percent compassionate, and we can access this compassion through cultivating the mode of transcendental goodness through Krishna Consciousness. In Krsna book, Srila Prabhupada explains this in the following way.

"When the demon was thus preparing to cut off his head, Lord Siva became very compassionate. This compassion is a symptom of the quality of goodness. Lord Siva is called tri-linga, "a mixture of the three material qualities." Therefore his manifestation of the nature of compassion is a sign of the quality of goodness. This compassion, however, is present in every living entity. The compassion of Lord Siva was aroused not because the demon was offering his flesh into the sacrificial fire but because he was about to commit suicide. This is natural compassion. Even if a common man sees someone preparing to commit suicide, he will try to save him. He does so automatically. There is no need to appeal to him. Therefore when Lord Siva appeared from the fire to check the demon from suicide, it was not done as a very great favor to him."[18]

18*Krsna, the Supreme Personality of Godhead*, chapter 88

Overwhelming Compassion

Overwhelming compassion means that the person who experiences this emotion or *bhava* of compassion so loves everyone that his actions are controlled by that love. Srila Prabhupada once related to us, "*When I think of how everyone in the world is suffering, it makes me cry. I actually cry.*" Prabhupada perfectly exhibited the overwhelming compassion of a pure devotee. He described it in Srimad-Bhagavatam.

> "*Pure devotees, out of compassion for the fallen souls, are kripalu, very kind to people in general; they distribute this Bhagavata knowledge all over the world. A kindhearted devotee is called dina-natha, protector of the poor, ignorant mass of people. Lord Krsna is also known as dina-natha or dina-bandhu, the master or actual friend of the poor living entities, and His pure devotee also takes the same position of dina-natha.*"19

In 1969, when I first read Krsna Book, I could not understand the philosophy of Krishna consciousness, yet I was irresistibly drawn by the spiritual energy that emanated from Srila Prabhupada's words. Once I had read about the little blue boy stealing butter and feeding it to the monkeys, I could not get the picture out of my mind, although I did not understand at that time who the little blue boy really was. When I encountered Srila Prabhupada for the first time in person, his loving mood of compassion overwhelmed me. He did not have to say anything for someone to feel this mood. I realized that – for the first time in my life – there was a person who loved me without demanding anything in return. I was able to feel his unconditional love. We know that a pure devotee unconditionally loves the Supreme Personality of Godhead, *ahaituki apratihata*, and that for this reason he loves all of Krishna's parts and parcels, without an ulterior motive. This is what convinced me to join the Krishna conscious movement. It was not the dress, hairstyle or anything else, but Prabhupada's great compassion and love.

Compassionate persons have the quality of *para-duhkha duhkhi*, which means they are ready to make personal sacrifices for the welfare of others. In other words, they consider others' happiness more important than their

---

19*Srimad-Bhagavatam* 4.12.51. purport

own. We cannot come to that platform overnight, but we can see it as one of our goals in spiritual life and pray to those who are on that platform.

Consider Srila Advaita Acarya's overwhelming compassion. He was thinking of everyone's welfare, and because of his compassion and prayers, Sri Caitanya Mahaprabhu appeared.

When Haridas Thakur was being whipped in twenty-two market places, he prayed for the people whipping him. He eventually made believe that he was dead so that the people whipping him would not get into trouble with their master.

Vasudeva Datta prayed to Lord Caitanya, "Let me stay in this material world forever and suffer for all the sins so that everbody can go back to the spiritual world." Lord Caitanya, who is Krishna Himself, called Vasudeva Datta compassion personified.

Lord Rama manifested that overwhelming compassion. Lord Ramachandra loved His wife Sita Devi but saw His citizens as being of equal importance. He regarded His duty towards the citizens as important as His duty towards her. It appears as if He was very cruel to His wife; however He saw everyone equally, not considering His personal interest in His wife. Therefore, He had to ask Sita Devi to leave the kingdom. Of course, there are also esoteric reasons for that. The Lord sent Sita Devi away in order for Them to experience the mood of *vipralambha-seva*, the mood of separation.

Lord Caitanya Mahaprabhu, the most munificent Personality of Godhead, left His wife and mother in the middle of the night in order to take *sannyasa*. Behind that too is an esoteric reason, but the external reason was to save the living entities. It was for everyone's sake that He left His young wife and set the example of sacrificing His own happiness.

A Well-wisher to All Living Entities

"He [the sadhu] is not only a well-wisher of human society, but a well-wisher of animal society as well. It is said here, sarva-dehinam, which indicates all living entities who have accepted material bodies. Not only does the human being have a material body, but other living entities, such as cats and dogs, also have material bodies. The devotee of the Lord is merciful to everyone —

the cats, dogs, trees, etc. He treats all living entities in such a way that they can ultimately get salvation from this material entanglement.

Sivananda Sena, one of the disciples of Lord Caitanya, gave liberation to a dog by treating the dog transcendentally. There are many instances where a dog got salvation by association with a sadhu, because a sadhu engages in the highest philanthropic activities for the benediction of all living entities."20

One should be able to feel compassion for souls beyond those in human bodies. You can try to make some connection with them. We are able to communicate with entities who cannot speak – animals and even plants. At one of my more advanced level seminars a student connected with grass. She described to me what the grass was feeling in the shade, out in the sun, and so on. This student actually developed empathy with grass. It is possible because we are all connected with Supersoul. Supersoul helps us to network with other living beings, communicating through our hearts.

Another of my workshop participants managed to empathically connect with the snails in her garden. Unhappy about the snails eating the vegetables she'd wanted to offer to Krishna, she collected all the snails from her garden and put them further away. By giving them a certain area where they could eat the vegetation, she connected with their needs

When I collect flowers for the *Govardhan silas* that I worship, I look to see if there are bugs on a flower I intend to pick. If so, I choose another flower instead. I don't want to unnecessarily disturb the bugs. We can feel compassion for living beings even simpler than bugs by meditating on the fact that, as spirit souls like us, they too are loved by Krishna and experience pains and pleasures in this world.

I once visited a pharmaceutical company that raises chlorella. Watching these single-cell green algae, it seemed to me that they were all communicating with each other. This is actually true. They live in small

---

20*Srimad-Bhagavatam* 3.25.21. purport

villages called colonies, and when something is going on somewhere else, they will group together. I asked a scientist working with the company, "How do these cells communicate with each other?" He said, "We do not know, but they do communicate with each other." They obviously don't have little algae computers with an algae internet, yet somehow or other they network with each other.

I went into a room in which the creatures were being examined under a microscope. They could be seen on a TV screen. Some algae were on the screen, and there was also a different being called paramecium. The lab people explained to me that the pH of the water was made higher in order to kill these other creatures. They said, "Those creatures are our enemies." And I was thinking, "Look at the consciousness they have." Of course, it is business consciousness, mode of passion consciousness, where you have friends and enemies. Sometimes in business one thinks like that. I was thinking, "How can you think in this way about Lord Krishna's creatures?!" Then I observed the paramecium moving all over the place eating the chlorella and thought, *jivo jivasya jivanam*, the bigger living entity eats the smaller living entity. I felt compassion for these algae being eaten and also for the predatory paramecium. Both of them were under the influence of the laws of nature and covered by the material energy.

Admittedly, it is easier to be empathic with more developed beings such as the four-legged animals – cats, dogs, horses – as they are similar to human beings. They are virtually the same as a child, and hitting them is the same as hitting a child. Some people subscribe to training dogs by hitting them and pushing their face into the stool. It may be that a dog becomes remorseful and obedient, but he will be fearful for the rest of his/her life.

Being compassionate towards animals not only manifests by causing no physical harm to them, but also attempting to help them in their spiritual progress. I've experienced animals having their own need for spirituality. Prior to coming to the Krishna conscious movement, I used to go into the forest to meditate and chant Om and Hare Krishna for six or eight hours a day. As I sat in a lotus position, animals would come up to me. At times I was surrounded by them, not bears or lions, of course, but smaller animals such as raccoons, rabbits, squirrels and the like. They usually don't come that close to humans, but they came very close to me, because they could sense the peace and spirituality. They are more covered than human beings, but their need for spirituality is definitely present. Lord Caitanya

Mahaprabhu was able to get them to dance and chant together. We can also chant Hare Krishna to animals, and to plants, and help them in their spiritual progress. Another good way of assisting them is to give them prasadam, as Srila Prabhupada elaborates in the following conversation.

> Srila Prabhupada: *Yes. If you have a garden and somebody says, "I want to eat some fruit," you'll say, "Yes, come on. Take as much fruit as you like." But, he should not gather more than he can eat and take it away. Any number of men can come and eat to their satisfaction. The farmers do not even prohibit the monkeys, "All right, let them come in. After all, it is God's property." This is the Krsna conscious system. If an animal, say a monkey, comes to your garden to eat, don't prohibit him. He is also part and parcel of Krsna. If you prohibit him, where will he eat?*
>
> *I have another story. This one was told by my father. My father's elder brother was running a cloth shop. Before closing the shop my uncle would put out a basin filled with rice. Of course, as in any village, there were rats. But, the rats would take the rice and not cut even a single cloth. Cloth is very costly. If even one cloth had been cut by a rat, then it would have been a great loss. So, with a few pennies' worth of rice, he saved many dollars' worth of cloth. This Krsna culture is practical. They are also part and parcel of God. Give them food. They'll not create any disturbance. Give them food.*
>
> *Everyone has an obligation to feed whoever is hungry - even if it is a tiger. Once, a certain spiritual teacher was living in the jungle. His disciples knew, "The tigers will never come and disturb us, because our teacher keeps some milk a little distance from the asrama, and the tigers come, drink and go away."* [21]

Please let us not forget our fellow human beings. It is sad when devotees spend a lot of time gently removing ants from the kitchen, one by one, but do not deal nicely with one another. We humans are also tiny sparks of the

---

[21] Room conversation – June 11, 1974, Paris

31

same Person that brings forth the ants, and we deserve the same care and compassion that they do.

Emotions

We often hear emotions being decried as illusion or in devotee lingo, *maya*, but they are an integral part of ourselves. Advanced spiritual study is centered on the study of emotions (*bhavas*). The spiritual realm is the realm of *bhavas*. I do not claim to be experiencing these advanced stages but I'm definitely interested in being fully compassionate. And compassion is not just a theoretical or philosophical concept. It involves emotions.

For example, the reason for my not taking milk products or any other animal-based foods is that I can't take them. I choose the word "can't" because I am blocked by strong emotions - a sense of compassion, feelings, and ethics. The very thought of eating something that is connected with so much suffering (the cruelty accompanying milk production in modern dairies) intensifies my sorrow for these other entities to such an extent that I find myself frozen with grief. When I explained this during a class in Croatia, some remarked that they had never thought of it in this way before. I suggested to them that they get in touch with themselves and with their own feelings, not only with regard to this subject but to all other aspects of their lives as well.

Some devotees may disagree with my view of emotions because of the negative connotation the topic of emotions evoke. Some may even express concern that people new to the process of Krishna consciousness will be encouraged to let their feelings guide their actions instead of functioning from the platform of intelligence. They may give an example to illustrate this point- a devotee who does not attend the morning program because, his emotions are telling him not to go. I explain, yes, emotions are an important aspect of ourselves and are not to be neglected. At the same time our intelligence is equally important and also not to be neglected. The question is how to reconcile conflicts between the emotions and intelligence.

One should recognize that emotions do not exist by themselves. They are products of needs fulfilled or unfulfilled. Unpleasant emotions, such as anger, come from needs that are not being fulfilled and pleasant emotions, such as happiness, come from needs that are being fulfilled. One has to examine with intelligence to ascertain the needs unfulfilled or fulfilled that are the cause of one's emotions. Emotions originate within one's self in connection with needs. [Here I am using self in a broad sense to indicate the physical self as well as the spiritual self] Strategies for meeting needs may have to be revised, but that can best be done after a need gets recognized. As a case in point, my strong aversion toward eating animal products stems from my strong need for compassion.

Using my intelligence, I can see that the need for compassion and love is in harmony with my spiritual development, which is a need in itself. In fact, every basic need like sustenance, joy, interaction, play and interdependence is naturally in harmony with spirituality. When I experience an emotion, I examine it with my intelligence in order to connect it with its need. In this way I can make sure to use the proper productive strategy for meeting my needs, and ultimately become completely Krishna conscious, as my foremost need is to love Krishna. That is the only thing that will ever completely satisfy my soul.

I reveal my feelings and thoughts regarding being compassionate toward animals because it is important for me to be open and honest.

As far as the example I gave concerning the devotee who does not attend the morning program because his emotions are telling him not to, I would advise him to engage his intelligence to analyze where those emotions are coming from in terms of his underlying needs. It could be that his need for autonomy (making one's own choices) is causing him to not want to go to the morning program. He values his ability to make choices on his own.

This is a good thing. Prabhupada wanted us to be independently thoughtful. But the strategy that this devotee is using for satisfying these needs cannot accomplish its purpose and will moreover, leave other essential needs unmet. Rebellion destroys our autonomy, as we are still controlled by negativity towards the person or institution which we are rebelling against. Of course, that control is negative. Rebellion is a non-productive strategy for achieving autonomy, because one only accomplishes the opposite. To make it worse, rebellion in this example prevents other basic needs such as spiritual advancement, happiness (arising from spiritual awareness), joy, and interdependence, from being fulfilled. Therefore, the result of this devotee's strategy of rebellion will be misery. Nevertheless, their rebellion is entirely understandable. On the way to becoming emotionally free (autonomous) the intermediate stage after moving away from submission, is that of "rebellion" or "obnoxiousness."

This is a natural stage that routinely occurs among those beginning to break free. You will find this with children when they grow up, beginning with the stage called the "terrible twos." Before this age they totally identified with their mother or other caregivers. At around two years of age they begin to assert their individuality. If they receive empathy during this stage the children quickly develop as individuals. But if instead, there is opposition – even the use of the term "terrible twos" is not productive – they become more and more rebellious and will likely, later in life, face serious challenges such as inexplicable anger issues. I have seen this in domination-type cultures in which children are forced to conform under the threat of punishment, or when they are controlled through rewards.

I think most of us can recognize these domination cultural effects either within our own religious society or within broader social groups. If the person is given encouragement, help, and empathy during the rebellious stage, they can reach a natural stage of emotional liberation, in which they are in touch with authentic needs and therefore function as a contributing member of society.

Empathic awareness and communication can be used as a powerful tool to liberate ourselves and our society from the conditioning and abuse of power that ignores emotions, feelings, and needs. Otherwise, the social dynamic we perpetuate will be one that is unable to contribute or support a fully spiritual life.

CHAPTER TWO

Disconnection in Communication

If it is our true nature to be connected and compassionate, how and why did we become disconnected? Judgmental language, domination cultures, blaming patterns, authoritarianism, a ritualistic mentality, emotional repression, promises of reward, and threats of punishment are just some of the reasons we are disconnected from ourselves and others. We will examine how the structures of society contribute to this disconnection by encouraging violence, and the misuse of power within relationships. It's crucial that we learn to connect empathically and work to fully integrate compassion into our lives.

Judgmental Language

When we judge someone, or criticize other people's activities or mentality, we use judgmental language. One of the main reasons why we disconnect either within the Krishna consciousness movement or outside of it, is that we are accustomed to using judgmental labels. Judgmental statements generally utilize some form of the verb "to be" – "You are a rascal, ruffian, offensive." "She is spaced out, in maya, lazy, mental, sentimental, useless, just a mataji."

Interestingly, "positive" labels won't help us to connect either, because as living entities we are not static. It is vital to understand that. We are Krishna's energy, and when we dispense designations such as the ones above, it fosters differences between people and creates splits within our own self.

The most beneficial phrases we can use are those based on eternal truths: "We are part and parcel of Krishna. We are devotees of Krishna." Temporary labels are *upadis* or designations and do not help us in our Krishna consciousness. They merely disconnect us.

One academic study concluded that the more a society uses static labels, the more the members in that society are prone to violence. The many Balkan conflicts were exacerbated by the use of static labels. Seeing others as a designation, such as Bosnian, Serbian, Croatian, Slovenian, Catholic, Muslim etc., created jarring divisions between people which eventually exploded into violence. So, what is judgmental language exactly?

It is language that gives the impression that someone is either "right" or "wrong" based on their actions, and also a judgment that indicates someone's nature is either "bad" or "good". There are endless labels – words – we can use to support this. It is language that puts people into boxes or groups and also divides, as in the "us" or "them"; enemy or friend mentality. It completely ignores the needs of another, based on externalities, without considering what might be the internal need based motive. It is also language that is based on external "moralistic" judgments rather than being "value-based". In other words, we place a label on others without considering the fact that perhaps they have different needs than us, value things differently than we do and experience things differently than us.

An example of an external judgment is: "Women are ignorant."

Domination Culture

A domination culture demands certain actions in order for one to be rewarded or to avoid punishment. When a student is judged based on his/her school grades this indicative of a domination culture as he/she will be rewarded or punished for his/her actions. The endless stream of killings shown on TV and in movies teach us to see violence as a practical means to achieve one's goals. A danger of engaging in violence towards ourselves or towards life (by demanding, controlling, blaming, overworking, stimulating feelings of guilt, etc.) is that it invites some form of a violent reaction from life (accident, disease, depression, etc.)

Maintaining a domination-type culture requires the use of a corresponding nomenclature. Language supports culture, and culture supports language. When people hear demands, they have one of two reactions, either submission or rebellion. Neither one is good, inclusive of submission which is usually done because of some sort of fear.

Of great interest, in that regard, is that prolonged exposure to a hierarchical situation – which in other words is called a domination culture – raises the risk of losing one's heart connection and being caught up in 'shoulds' and 'musts.' In ISKCON, like any other institution, we sometimes find the tendency to legislate relationships, which can easily destroy the heart of relationships. We often forget that Krishna consciousness is meant to be nurtured by the heart.

The domination culture adopted by some in ISKCON hinders the development of Krishna consciousness. It's important to render service or perform *sadhana* not because we think we *have to* or hope to gain something material from it – recognition for instance – rather we should *choose to,* because we genuinely have the desire to make loving offerings to Krishna and His devotees. We can best serve when we feel deeply connected and have a sense of joy in doing so; freely choosing to serve instead of because it is our duty. We can best perform our duties in the context of listening to and following the spiritual desire within our hearts.

The alternative to exerting power over others, as is being done in most religious societies, is to cooperate with others. This is what Prabhupada said he wanted. He taught that our love for him will be tested by our love for and cooperation with each other.

Blaming

At each level of ISKCON management we may find devotees blaming those on the level just above them for their problems. A cook in the temple may, for example, blame the temple commander, who blames the vice president, who blames the president and who, in turn, blames the GBC or the guru.

When blaming situations prevail, it indicates that we need better training for those in leadership positions. Well-trained leaders will perform their service nicely and not cause those under them to feel chronically dissatisfied. In order for persons with responsibility to act effectively, good training is required. No one will argue with that, although this hierarchical blaming of others is due to more than merely a lack of training. It indicates a culture of disempowerment, in which we look to others because we are overly dependent.

Prabhupada wanted devotees to become independently thoughtful and resourceful- that is to be brahmanas. He often mentioned the brahmana Canakya: "*This is India's heritage. Canakya Pandita was the greatest scholar and politician. He was the prime minister of Maharaja Emperor Candragupta. Chanakya Puri in New Delhi is named after Canakya Pandita. He was living in a cottage, not accepting any salary. And as soon as Maharaja Candragupta wanted some explanation for an instruction Canakya had given him, Canakya resigned. Such detachment is the standard of persons born in India."* A true brahmana is not controlled by money, rewards, perks, position, power, guilt, blame or threats. Their only interest is in the absolute truth and spiritual advancement.

Srila Prabhupada presented Krishna consciousness in a pure, loving way. When we become influenced by the modes of nature, we present Krishna consciousness in a way that is either passionate, ignorant or in the material mode of goodness. In Srimad Bhagavatam Lord Kapila describes passionate Krishna consciousness in these words: *"The worship of Deities in the temple by a separatist, with a motive for material enjoyment, fame and opulence, is devotion in the mode of passion."*22

Ignorant Krishna consciousness is presented by Lord Kapila as follows: *"Devotional service executed by a person who is envious, proud, violent and angry, and who is a separatist, is considered to be in the mode of darkness."*23

Further, Lord Kapila delineates Krishna consciousness in the material mode of goodness: *"When a devotee worships the Supreme Personality of Godhead and offers the results of his activities in order to free himself from the inebrieties of fruitive activities, his devotion is in the mode of goodness."*24

Finally, Lord Kapila speaks of transcendental Krishna consciousness: *"The manifestation of unadulterated devotional service is exhibited when one's mind is at once attracted to hearing the transcendental name and qualities of the Supreme Personality of Godhead, who is residing in everyone's heart. Just as the water of the Ganges flows naturally down towards the ocean, such devotional ecstasy, uninterrupted by any material condition, flows towards the Supreme Lord."*25

Therefore, devotees in the Krishna consciousness movement should constantly strive to guide everyone towards transcendental devotional service. When we use rewards, guilt, threats, punishments, etc., we

---

22 *Srimad Bhagavatam 3.29.8.*

23 *Srimad Bhagavatam 3.29.9.*

24 *Srimad Bhagavatam 3.29.10.*

25 *Srimad Bhagavatam 3.29.11.*

propagate devotional service being performed in the modes of material nature. Pure devotional service is motivated by love alone.

Sometimes our authorities tell us that unless we obey them, we will go to the hellish planets! Apart from the dubious veracity of that statement, we should understand that goading people on with the fear of hell automatically shifts them into the mode of ignorance or passion. Other religious groups regularly do this as well. I can't estimate how many times I've been told that unless I surrendered to a particular religious group I would be going to hell. Of course, I would usually retort along the lines of, "That is quite wonderful! I'll be able to serve God by preaching in Hell. All the souls there will be very receptive." After hearing this, the person who had attempted to scare me would often back off and slink away.

If we give in a way that is attentive to needs, it will nurture a voluntary spirit of love in others' hearts. There is a revealing quote by Prabhupada about the voluntary spirit of devotion and the leaders' duty to encourage it.

> *"So, the future of this Krishna Consciousness movement is very bright, so long the managers remain vigilant that 16 rounds are being chanted by everyone without fail, that they are all rising before four o'clock in the morning, attending mangal arati. Our leaders shall be careful not to kill the spirit of enthusiastic service, which is individual, spontaneous and voluntary. They should try always to generate some atmosphere of fresh challenge to the devotees, so that they will agree enthusiastically to rise and meet it. That is the art of management, to draw out spontaneous loving spirit of sacrificing some energy for Krishna. But, where are so many expert managers?*
>
> *All of us should become expert managers and preachers. We should not be very much after comforts and become complacent or self-contented. There must be always some tapasya, strictly observing the regulative principles. Krishna Consciousness movement must be always a challenge, a great achievement to be gained by voluntary desire to do it, and that will keep it healthy.*

So, you big managers now try to train up more and more some competent preachers and managers like yourselves."26

How shall we motivate others and, even more importantly, how do we motivate ourselves? We motivate ourselves and others through the voluntary spirit of pleasing Krishna and His representatives. This voluntary spirit will awaken a real sense of Bhakti in our hearts.

Someone asked me how we can perform our duties joyfully, even those that are not among our favorites. I answered that we should strive to understand that we are choosing to do those activities, not that we "have" to do them. Actually, there is nothing that we "have" to do. We have a choice in every instance. Let's take chanting as an example. If we think that we have to chant, then our chanting will become drudgery, but when we think we are choosing to chant, the chanting becomes much easier and joyful as well. We will benefit from constantly motivating ourselves internally by actively using the words "I choose."

To encourage others, we utilize requests, rather than demands. A devotee once said to me, "You have to do this!" My mind immediately rebelled against doing what he demanded, although the task itself was quite reasonable. I did what he demanded but my mind was screaming, "No, no no!" Had he said, "Would you be willing to do this, because we need …?" I would have jumped at the opportunity.

One has to take the time to explain, and in management situations sometimes we feel so pressed for time, that we don't take that important step

Simply saying "please" and "thank you" can be very effective. Of course, one must mean "please" and "thank you" rather than just mouthing the words and giving the opposite message by their tone of voice and body language.

Choosing

I don't have much taste for management. My nature is to engage in helping others chant, hear Krishna's pastimes and so forth. So, I started to

---

26 *Letter to: Karandhara-- Bombay 22 December, 1972*

adopt an attitude of "why do I *have to* attend meetings?" I was beginning to have negative feelings about these meetings, and experience them as being very unpleasant. Then I remembered that I had choices in life. No one was forcing me to do anything. I didn't have to do anything. I analyzed my real reason (value) for attending the meetings. It was to please Srila Prabhupada. This immediately shifted my train of thought towards, "I choose to go to the meetings as an act of devotion to Prabhupada and Radha-Krishna." As soon as I rephrased things in this way, the meetings became part of my practice of *bhakti*, and I would relish a devotional mellow while attending them. This does not mean that I'm now in love with management – far from it – but the point is that I am choosing to do something as an act of love even though it is not easy, which changes the entire mood from chore to devotion.

When we function from a conscious desire and need to love, even something that would not ordinarily be pleasant becomes so, because of the *bhakti rasa* that is there. We should try to eliminate any ideas that we "have" to do something or are "supposed" to do something.

I received an email from a sincere disciple. She mentioned that the other devotees in the temple were cautioning her not to expect devotional service to be equally ecstatic after performing it for years. They told her that she was just experiencing "newbie" happiness, and that after a while this happiness and enthusiasm would fade away. I wondered why that should be the experience of so many devotees, and how we can maintain the enthusiasm we've felt as new devotees and even increase that enthusiasm! Krishna consciousness does gets better and better with time. That has indeed been my experience. Considering this, I came to understand that one can lose his experience of ecstasy not only as a consequence of offenses, but, in the case of most devotees, because of the ritualistic mentality that many develop over time.

This is the result of being motivated to do things because we are 'supposed' to do them. We 'have' to do them. With an outlook like that, everything – starting with *mangala arati* moving forward – turns into a huge burden. When you are *supposed* to do something, your mind views it as something you would *not* do unless you *had* to do it.

The way I remain enthusiastic is to take the time to think before I do something for Krishna, such as attending the morning program, chanting rounds and performing a service. I make the effort to remember how truly fortunate I am to receive the mercy of Krishna and Srila Prabhupada, and how kind they are to let me do those things in spite of my not being qualified to do them. I mentally thank Krishna and Prabhupada for permitting me to serve them like this. I then think, "Wow, I am really going to have a great time doing mangala arati, Deity worship, chanting, serving, etc. I'm really looking forward to it! I can hardly wait." In this way, I build up my expectancy for exuberance and enthusiasm. It is not an artificial ruse, because these activities really are, *kevala ananda kanda* (simply blissful).

The reason we don't feel blissful is not because the activities are lacking in some way, but rather we allow the mentality of *being forced* to enter our consciousness. When I perform service for Krishna, I seek to cultivate the mood of joyfulness and thankfulness along with full awareness of what I am doing and for "Whom" I am doing it. When I chant a prayer in Sanskrit, I mentally and sometimes even verbally (under my breath) recite the translation as well. Try this for yourself during the *aratis, Tulasi* worship, *Guru-puja*, etc. You too, may find that doing so brings out a whole new dimension, and before long you will feel like jumping in ecstasy.

Authority and Emotional Dependency

In my travels, I've encountered many devotees hurting from the effects of emotional dependency or attempting to free themselves from emotional dependency.

Emotional dependency can affect GBCs, gurus, presidents, authorities, *sannyasis*, preachers, disciples, *brahmacaris*, *gurukulis*, husbands, wives, *vanaprasthas*, women, children; really everyone. The symptoms of emotional dependency differ from person to person but often include depression, anxiety, heartaches, over dependency, regressive traits, anger, headaches, backaches, etc.

There are two main categories of emotionally dependent personalities in a society. One is the dominant authority figure, and the other is the person who is emotionally dependent on that authority figure. Both personality types suffer under the pressures of this dynamic. One may further be emotionally dependent on an institution, and the institutional paradigms may foster and perpetuate this dependency. In hierarchical institutions, there is a greater presence of tendency towards emotional bondage.

A person in a position of authority assumes responsibility for persons hierarchically under him or her. This is a paternal situation. When the subordinate person does not live up to the institutionalized expectations, the authority sometimes experiences it as a personal failing, much in the same way that parents regard a child's disappointing performance as their personal failure. Such a dynamic might be useful for some time when it involves parents and a child, but between two adults it typically leads to negative mental and physical repercussions; for both the authority figure assuming responsibility and for the subordinate.

Early in the relationship the authority figure is attached to or focused on the notion of being responsible for the dependent's emotional, spiritual, or material well-being. Then, when the dependent acts or thinks in ways contrary to the authority's concept of well-being, the authority could feel guilt ("It's my fault"), anger, or a variety of other emotions. When that authority has dominion over multiple living entities and persists in the assumption of being responsible in every respect for matters entirely outside of his or her control-the experience that results from carrying the emotional burden of guilt and inappropriate caring will likely be exhaustion, if not illness.

Next, the authority is liable to enter what I previously called the rebellious stage, in which they categorically reject responsibility for the dependents and will not even want to talk to them. Meanwhile, the dependents, too, may go through successive stages. Many people will enthusiastically enter into a relationship with the implicit promise that others will be cared for in ways to which only a child should be entitled. It takes great strength of character to be independently thoughtful, as Srila Prabhupada wants us to be. *"...Krishna Consciousness Movement is for training men to be independently thoughtful."*27

While being cared for in this way may feel "warm and fuzzy" at first, it ultimately leads to the dysfunction of losing one's self esteem and self-confidence. In fact, it can be seen as the atrophy of a vital part of the dependent's very being. What usually occurs in the course of time is that the dependent person becomes dissatisfied with the care they are receiving, and steadily grows needier. When the unrealistic expectations are tied to unrecognized and unfulfilled needs which are not met, the dependent person can become despondent and reject the care altogether; often labeling the caregiver as an enemy.

There are many examples of devotees who feel negatively about ISKCON and its authorities to an extent that exceeds the parameters of "normal" emotional functioning. They suffer from extreme disappointment about ISKCON's failure to care for them as an institution in which the representatives had, to their understanding, implicitly promised to offer. Publically criticising ISKCON they may state they are only helping ISKCON to better fulfill its responsibilities, but in fact it is a process for them to vent emotional frustrations that may predate, sometimes by decades, any contact they've had with ISKCON.

To effectively and empathically deal with this challenge, there is a need to clearly define the relationship between authority figures and dependents. An authority figure (individual or institution) benefits by refraining from implicitly or explicitly promising to meet all the needs of a prospective dependent. It is more productive to assume the role of a facilitator, committed to helping others understand how to fulfill their own needs by taking responsibility as an autonomous human being. This will be a hard

---

27 *Prabhupada's Letter to: Karandhara -- Bombay 22 December, 1972*

nut to crack in light of the entrenched view that a religious society's effective and efficient functioning can only be based upon strictly enforced obedience. Some may think that promoting this objective of facilitating individual autonomy will result in losing control of our society.

There are also emotional objections stemming from addiction to followers' adulation and desire to increase the numbers of followers. It is good if we can remember and realize that Lord Caitanya in His *Siksastaka* cautioned us about this addiction.

In my experience, however, it is not that our society will disintegrate when we encourage individual autonomy. Quite the contrary. Whenever devotees are encouraged to develop their individuality and to serve joyfully, not because they have to, they function at a higher level of enthusiasm, efficiency, and even responsibility to the society. Better yet, their joyfulness attracts more and more people, inspiring them to render voluntary service too. They will feel safe to use their imagination fully to come up with ever more dynamic ways of sharing Krishna consciousness with the multitude of conditioned *jiva* souls.

To achieve emotional freedom on all levels of our society a paradigm shift is required. By doing this we will feel as if a great weight has been lifted from our shoulders. Much strength will have to be mustered though, if people are to be responsible for their own lives, and authorities for renouncing subtle temptations to control people's lives.

There is a fundamental difference between fear of authority and respect for authority. We should understand that difference, and strive towards respectful dealings rather than fearful ones. There is nothing wrong with authority. The authority though should be earning respect rather than demanding respect and obedience.

Respect is earned in three major ways.

1) Someone knows or can accomplish what others don't know or cannot accomplish.

2) Others regard these as valuable assets because their lives are enriched by them.

3) Others see that these assets are being offered and shared by those who possess them.

Fear has been built into many of our cultural structures – parent/child, guru/disciple, GBC/devotee, manager/employee. Our current prevalent culture functions by imposing a system of rewards and punishments so that people can be made to behave, to be obedient.

Think about how fear can limit our living and acting authentically.

In order for trust to be alive, it is necessary for those in positions of authority to earn any respect "due" them, and great caution should be taken to not "become" their title; losing their sense of humanness and distorting their perception of themselves or others. Currently society obtains obedience by making others submit through punishment or reward. Voluntary cooperation takes trust, not coercion. Trust is gained when there is a situation that is free from fear.

People under an authority must be careful not to esteem those in positions of authority merely on account of their titles, or think that they have to submit because of these titles. It's best if leaders don't hide that they also have feelings, nor misrepresent themselves as being their designation. Srila Prabhupada never implied he was better than others, rather he saw himself as a servant, even of those subordinate to him. It is in our best interest that those in positions of authority never imply (adopt the mentality) that they are better than those whom they lead. Misused authority has the power to destroy what is "alive" in us – the desire to serve.

When a devotee asks the guru to solve their problem, the guru avoids doing it since this is the devotee's challenge and dilemma. The guru will give hints and advice, but he will avoid solving the problem. If the guru were to actually resolve the issue, the devotee would come again and again and never understand the need for taking responsibility. And, should the method that the guru used to solve the problem not work, the guru may feel guilty for failing his disciple, or the disciple may blame the guru for a failed resolution. The guru can only guide devotees to solve their problems for themselves.

Independence

It is necessary to clarify what I mean by independence. I do not mean independence from Krishna. No one is independent from Krishna. The thought that one ever could be independent is but *Maya*, illusion. However, as personalists we recognize that each of us is an independent *jiva* soul. We are *not* all one. We are individual beings, eternally part and parcel of Krishna. That is our ontological position.

It is interesting how independence plays out both in the eternal sense and in the context of manifesting *bhakti* in this world. We cannot be forced or cajoled into rendering service to Krishna. It is a purely voluntary act of the heart, and that is the essential aspect of *bhakti*.

In an institutional setting we too often lose this understanding of the soul's free will and try to force people into Krishna consciousness, using expressions such as "you must," "you have to," "you are supposed to," "Don't be in *maya*, Prabhu." "I am your authority, and you have to listen to me!" "Shut up and act properly!" "If you don't do this Krishna will punish you." "You're going to get a heavy reaction for this, or for not doing this." "If you don't do this, I will be highly disappointed in you." "You are causing me grief." These express emotionally and mentally manipulative techniques that actually separate the person from real *bhakti*, and may ultimately result in someone acquiring distaste for devotional service.

Krishna says in the Bhagavat Gita: *"This knowledge is the king of education, the most secret of all secrets. It is the purest knowledge, and because it gives direct perception of the self by realization, it is the perfection of religion. It is everlasting, and it is joyfully performed."*28

For something to be done joyfully, it must be done voluntarily. A person must retain his or her sense of individuality, freedom of choice, and autonomy – otherwise there is no love. There is no love without a lover and a beloved. When we function on the platform of blind obedience, we have done away with one of the two. I've found that we do have individual needs in spiritual life and even in the spiritual world. Our need

---

28 *Bhagavat Gita* 9.2.

for autonomy is one of those needs that should be met both in the arena of devotional practice and in the eternal life of devotional perfection. Our autonomy is, of course, never absolute. It is always relative. The only person who has absolute autonomy is Krishna (He is *svarat*). That said, leaders have to be very careful to avoid killing the voluntary service mood of any individual by imposing too much authority.

Srila Prabhupada was very much against centralization. Here is a significant quote from Srila Prabhupada on this issue.

> *"Regarding your points about taxation, corporate status, etc., I have heard from Jayatirtha, you want to make big plan for centralization of management, taxes, monies, corporate status, book keeping, credit, like that. I do not at all approve of such plan. Do not centralize anything. Each temple must remain independent and self-sufficient. That was my plan from the very beginning, why you are thinking otherwise? Once before you wanted to do something centralizing with your GBC meeting and if I did not interfere the whole thing would have been killed. Do not think in this way of big corporation, big credits, centralization, these are all nonsense proposals.*
>
> *Only thing I wanted was that books printing and distribution should be centralized, therefore I appointed you and Bali Mardan to do it. Otherwise, management, everything, should be done locally by local men. Accounts must be kept, things must be in order and lawfully done, but that should be each temple's concern, not yours.*
>
> *Krishna Consciousness Movement is for training men to be independently thoughtful and competent in all types of departments of knowledge and action, not for making bureaucracy.*
>
> *Once there is bureaucracy, the whole thing will be spoiled. There must be always individual striving and work and responsibility, competitive spirit, not that one shall dominate and distribute benefits to the others, and they do nothing but beg from you and you provide. No. Never mind there may be botheration to register each centre, take tax certificate each, and become separate corporations in each state. That will train men how to do these*

things, and they shall develop reliability and responsibility, that is the point."29

It is my firm belief that Prabhupada not only wanted temple presidents to be autonomous, but that he intended the same principles to apply to individual devotees. So, the business of leaders is to guide people to Krishna's lotus feet and to facilitate their individual expressions of *bhakti*. To guide does not mean to push (through threats, guilt, etc.) but to pull by the attraction of a good example, and compassion.

---

29 *Letter to: Karandhara -- Bombay 22 December, 1972*

Communication that Blocks Compassion

There are many blocks to our communication – among these are criticizing, blaming, insulting, demanding, punishing, rewarding, and fixing others. These produce guilt, shame and depression. Marshall B. Rosenberg (Ph.D.) has shared some common behaviors that block our ability to be empathic, which in turn prevents us from being able to connect with someone. The following are some examples for reference.

Advising: "My advice is that you (do, say, try) it like this …"
One-upping: "Interesting. You should hear what happen to me "
Educating: "Think about it as a lesson learned; you should …"
Consoling: "Don't worry. You did the best you could under the circumstances."
Story telling: "Oh wow, really? That reminds me of …"
Shutting down:."Oh well, that's life."
Interrogating:."Really? Who said so? When? Where were you? Why did they say that?"
Explaining: "I'm sorry. I meant to…, but this and this and this…"
Correcting:."No that's not right. You don't remember, it was actually like…"
But-ting: "Maybe, *but* you should have"

It is helpful to distinguish between the problems that belong to us and the problems belonging to other persons. Many times, we take on other people's problems and make them our own. To avoid this tendency, one can mentally check to see if something is our own problem or that of another person. Suppose we are sharing our room with another devotee who snores and we can't sleep. Is this our problem or the other person's problem? It is definitely our problem, because we are the ones unable to sleep while the other person is sleeping soundly. Of course, the other person may have a health issue, but that is a separate issue.

In another instance, you are the temple president, and one of the devotees in your temple is feeling discouraged. Does this affect you or the devotee? It affects the devotee, because you may not even know that they feel discouraged. So, it is the other person who owns the problem.

Objectively identifying who owns the problem doesn't mean that we avoid offering help. By making the distinction of ownership we can help the other person in the best way by seeing things objectively and without judgment, by observing.

If an authority tends to take on other people's problems, it will only invite the others to become dependent on him and invite a cycle of dysfunction. As was mentioned earlier, Srila Prabhupada encouraged us to be independently thoughtful, which can be done by clearly understanding where the problem resides and offering support not ownership. Studies have indicated that people who take many problems upon themselves often get horrible back pain. Keep in mind that taking on others' problems has the potential to make us very sick.

In general, as far as problems are concerned, I like to rephrase them as challenges, and opportunites.

The Four D's of Disconnection

Know that what you say will have an impact. Take time to listen and to really hear. We will deal with four different ways in which deep communication is shut down: diagnosing, denying, demanding and deserving.

* Diagnosing *

Diagnoses are statements or thoughts that measure "goodness" or "badness." This can result in a very superficial view of others (and even ourselves) and make connecting and meeting needs nearly difficult. When we look at people (including ourselves) through the lens of designations, when we use labels, it disconnects us from having an empathic understanding. If we can avoid diagnosing ourselves and others, we will remove that block to communication.

Temple devotees on occasion look down on others whose lives have taken them outside of the sheltered temple environment. It's extremely important to consciously forego using language that promotes division. We have many designations in ISKCON that create division not only between our members and outsiders, but within ISKCON too: devotees/non-devotees, devotees/demons, devotees/raksasas, devotees/*karmis*, advanced devotees/sense gratifiers, etc. Several studies have shown that the more a culture uses divisive language, the more that culture will experience internal and external conflicts that easily flare up into violent confrontation.

A direct correlation exists between the incidence of violence and the use of judgmental language. Taking this to heart, I prefer to think of people who aren't practicing Krishna consciousness as "aspiring devotees." They just don't know yet that they are aspirants. They aspire in the sense that they do want Krishna, but they are just not aware of wanting Him. They are innocents. According to our philosophy the *madhyama adhikari* should regard those not opposed to Krishna consciousness as innocents. Reflecting on their innocence and unconscious desire for Krishna makes them the objects of compassionate thinking and action.

Exercise

Transform the following statements from judgments, to stating the facts and considering an underlying need looking to be fulfilled.

Examples

Original:."People who eat meat are demons."
Transformed:."When I see others eating meat I feel immensely sad and frustrated. Sad that the animal has to suffer so much pain, and frustrated that people who eat meat aren't considering the suffering involved."

Transform the following statements -

a. "That devotee is so harsh. She always yells when she wants you to do something."
b. "The temple president is very inconsiderate. They never ask my opinion."
c. "This devotee is so vain, they think they do everything right."

Words shape our consciousness. When we say something judgmental, or diagnose someone, our words have the potential to stimulate emotions that weren't there previously, whereas when we say something supportive or encouraging to someone, our words can create an empathetic connection, for us and for them. Try to remember that the more judgmental language is used, the more violence will take place.

* Denying Responsibility *

Denying responsibility means that we are not taking responsibility for our own feelings and emotions. We'll either throw our feelings onto others or expect them to fulfill our needs. We usually resort to using language that places the blame outside of ourselves. For example, "You made me do it! It's your fault that I'm miserable!" We spend much of our life doing what we think we "have to" do.

Try to do your service with a sense of joy and play– not fear, guilt, shame or obligation. There is tremendous value in being able to liberate ourselves from all this conditioning and misuse of power that denies our feelings and needs, and ultimately disconnects us from Krishna and his parts and parcels.

Exercise

Make a list of some examples of devotional activities you "have to do." Then take a minute to rephrase them as, "I choose to . . . because I want/need/value . . ."

Examples

"I did it because I *had* to do it."
"My overeating is just genetic, there's nothing I can do."
"I did it because my parent (boss, teacher, officer, etc.) said to."
"I drink because everyone else does it."
"I yelled at her because she was not acting properly."
"I have to work because everyone is depending on me."

The best solution is to drop the tendency to diagnose and judge others and instead, respect others, be attentive and empathic, and above all, learn to function on the platform of intelligence. Going back to what was shared earlier, *choosing* to do something allows for an introspective assessment and awareness of what is motiving our feelings and the needs underneath. This will allow for the freedom and intelligence to do things positively in our devotional service for Krishna.

* Demanding *

Demanding language communicates that if others don't comply, they are going to be punished or blamed somehow. There are many instances of our articulating our wishes as demands, especially when we hold a position of relative authority. A demand implies the threat of punishment, criticism or blame, and tends to result in reactions based on fear, guilt and shame. A request is something we make from the heart and with empathy for the feelings and needs of our listener.

Remember, when we demand something from another person, there are two possible reactions. One of them is that the person won't do it or fights against it. The other is that the person might do what we demand but will not feel happy about it, and after some time of doing these things without happiness, the person may explode emotionally usually due to a need for understanding or need to be heard, or perhaps they will feel depressed. On the other side of the equation, when someone doesn't do something we demand, we will often feel angry or try to make them feel guilty, or make their life miserable.

If you were to ask someone to do something for you, how would it sound as a demand and how would it sound as a request? Following are some examples that show the transformation of a demand into a request.

Examples

Demand language: "You *have* to clean your room. As long as you live in my house you have to follow my rules!"
Request language: "Would you be willing to keep your room clean this month, I don't have extra time to help clean it right now?"

Demand language: "Idiot! Don't drive like that – you'll get us killed!"
Request language: "When you drive twenty miles over the speed limit I feel really uncomfortable and unsafe, would you be willing to drive the speed limit when I'm with you?"

The distinction between a *demand* and a *request* is discernible by observing how the person asking for something reacts when the expressed wish is not fulfilled. For instance, when people did not do what Prabhupada wanted, he still remained loving and merciful. Because Prabhupada's love was unconditional, what might have sounded like a demand was not really a demand. It was more of a request. It is not so much the words that are important, but the intent. It is important to keep in mind that the guru may sometimes demand from us or diagnose us. But, because there is a loving relationship between guru and disciple, the disciple can understand why the guru is doing this.

* Deserving *

When we think that certain actions deserve certain rewards or punishments, we have been conditioned to believe that we'll get what we "deserve." For example, if we work hard, we deserve to make money and spend it how we like. If we break the law, we deserve to be punished. When we think we are not getting what we deserve, we tend to disconnect from our unmet needs and lapse into blame or criticism. This type of language communicates that if others do not comply, they will be blamed or punished. "They must learn that if they don't do what I say, there will be a price to pay!" On the other side of the same coin, rewards discourage risk-taking and motivate us by the reward rather than an intrinsic value of an action. It is important to do things from the heart, not out of fear, duty or for reward. In this regard, Marshall Rosenberg cites an example he observed in an airport, and eventually asked a mother, "How do you get your son to behave so well?" She responded, "I've found that in order to get children to do what you want, you need a smacker and a cracker."

Smacker (paddle) = punishment for bad behavior
Cracker = reward for good behavior

This is dog obedience school! When we use punishment, people obey, but at the cost of trust. This creates an aversion towards the activity, and others will begin to avoid us.

CHAPTER THREE

Applying Empathic Communication in Depth

Empathic communication is a language and communication skill that allows our real nature to be expressed, helps us avoid impulsive reactions, and brings us in contact with our real needs and the needs of others. The process of empathic communication has four elements:

1. Observation:.Seeing something without making any type of judgments
2. Feelings:.Being aware of our feelings (not our thoughts) about the observation
3. Needs:.Connecting with our needs
4. Request: Learning and implementing strategies to fulfill these needs, without making demands

Note: These four steps can also be applied when facilitating or connecting with others. In this way:

1. Observation: Seeing something without making any type of judgments
2. Feelings: Helping others understand their feelings by facilitating them in coming to the understanding of what their feelings are, not by telling them what their feelings are.
3. Needs: Encourage them to find their underlying needs behind the feeling.
4. Request: Encouraging them to find productive strategies that will help fulfill the underlying needs without conflicting with other needs.

1st Component: *Observation*

When we make an observation, we need to be specific about who did or said what, where and when – without judgment, just the facts. It is important that we differentiate *evaluations* (judgments/labeling) from *observations* (facts). Empathic communication discourages 'static' generalizations – labels, judgments and generalized statements that ignore the person. These judgements are a manifestation of impersonalism and, apart from denying the other person's feelings and needs behind a given action, they actually ignore our needs and feelings if we express ourselves in this way.

An example is, "You're so lazy!" A clear observation would be, "You left dirty mop water in the bucket yesterday." You can see that by making a clear observation it allows the opportunity for dialogue versus just pointing the finger at someone. The first example will create enmity and a disconnection, whereas with the second statement, the other person has the opportunity to respond. "Oh, I know. I'm sorry but I had an appointment and had to leave early. There was no one around to ask for help, so I was hoping to do it this morning."

If you think about it, the person who stated, "You're so lazy!" isn't allowing for the opportunity to express their own feelings and needs either. For example, they could share instead, "I was at the temple all day and when I was leaving I noticed the mop bucket was full of dirty water. I felt really frustrated because I need things to be clean, and I was too tired to empty it." Empathic communication really allows for a clear picture of what each of us values in life.

Using 'static' words will disconnect us from the possibility of gaining understanding and support. Here are some examples of how language can get in the way of a clear observation.
> **Obvious**: "You're so *ignorant*!"
> **Subtle**: "It's really *inappropriate* for you to speak to me that way."

Think about these statements, and reflect on how you would feel after hearing them. There are also certain words like *never*, *ever*, *whenever*, *whatever*, and *always*, which can be used in an observation, but again it is how they are used that impacts how they will be received.

Examples of these used in a clear observation:

"My experience is that *whenever* Bhakta dasa speaks, he talks for 30 to 45 minutes."
"I don't remember you *ever* sharing with me where to put the preparations."

Examples of these used in an unclear observation that includes an evaluation (judgment):

> "You are *always* on the phone."
> "She *never* does anything at the temple."
> "They *never* do what I ask."

"He *seldom* cooks *nicely*."
"You *frequently* leave a *mess*."

Instead of transmitting compassion and empathy, these terms will often stimulate a defensive response when used. Even terms that seem to be positive or neutral such as "boss," "intelligent girl," or "good devotee" place a general label on others rather than seeing them as a multi-faceted individual. When you make an observation, use just the facts.

Here are some examples of interactions that may interfere with making a clear observation and which avoid taking personal responsibility for our own needs and feelings.

Pointing a judgment at someone else, not sharing facts, and avoiding personal responsibility (not acknowledging one's own personal feelings and needs) and placing the burden on others

> **Avoiding**:."They're *too* faithful."
> **Responsible:**."When I see them follow the instructions of their guru, I think of them as being too faithful."
> Verbs that have a judgmental tone, as well as adjectives (descriptive)

> **Avoiding**:."She's *patronizing*." / "He's *mean*."
> **Responsible**: "I think she complements every person she sees."
> Inferring that your own thoughts about someone else are absolute, especially regarding their values and actions

> **Avoiding**:."He will *never* learn to sing."
> **Responsible**: *I don't think* he'll ever learn to sing, or He said, "I'll never learn to sing."
> Presuming that you know someone's potential action, considering a given situation

> **Avoiding**:."I know him, if you take him to the store you won't be on time."
> **Responsible**:."If you take him to the store, I'm concerned you won't be on time."
> Neglecting to be specific when referring to others

Avoiding: "Men don't care about their appearance."
Responsible:."I haven't seen the gentleman next door in clean clothes.
Using situations to point out someone's ability or lack of ability (with hidden agenda/ evaluation/judgment)

Avoiding:."Bhakti dasi doesn't know how to cook."
Responsible:."Bhakti dasi has burned the breakfast offering three times this week."

Behind every circumstance, there is a reason; and behind every person there are feelings and needs. Reflect on how you can take responsibility to make communication personal and empathic, by making unbiased observations.

Exercise

See if you can tell which statements below are observations or evaluations, and why. The answers are at the bottom of the page (and can be covered if desired, as you work through the exercise).

1. "Dasi was ignoring me for no reason yesterday."
2. "Dasi didn't call last night to cancel the meeting."
3. "Dasa didn't ask my opinion about the prasadam after the event."
4. "Dasi is a nice devotee."
5. "Dasa works way too much."
6. "Dasa is manipulative."
7. "Dasi was here by 5:00 a.m. every day this week."
8. "Dasa rarely washes his hands before taking prasadam."
9. "Bhakta dasa told me, "You don't have any intelligence."
10. "The temple president complains when I talk to him."

Answers:

1. EVALUATION "For no reason" is an evaluation, and "ignoring" assumes knowledge of what another person is feeling; their motivation.
2. OBSERVATION clear observation
3. OBSERVATION clear observation
4. EVALUATION. "nice devotee" – not specific; generalization
5. EVALUATION. "too much" – personal point of view
6. EVALUATION. "manipulative" – needs to be more specific; static label
7. OBSERVATION. clear observation
8. EVALUATION. "rarely" – not specific enough
9. OBSERVATION. direct statement of someone
10. EVALUATION. "complains" – not specific; generalization

2nd Component: *Feelings*

There is a heavy cost to not expressing our feelings. Thus, if we 'protect' ourselves at the cost of empathically connecting with others, we avoid being vulnerable, thinking it to be the safest path. In actuality, by not sharing our vulnerability we forfeit the opportunity to resolve conflicts and build healthy communities.

It's important to understand that *feelings* are different from *thoughts*. We often use the word "feel" when we are actually referring to thoughts, therefore we get disconnected from our actual feelings and emotions. In order to live a life fully connected to our self and to others it's necessary to distinguish between the two.

In the following examples, it's easy to replace the *feeling* statements, with *think*:

   I *feel that* you are inconsiderate.
   I *feel like* I'm not qualified.
   I *feel as if* they are being unreasonable.
   I *feel* I am never appreciated.
   I *feel* it is a complete loss.
   I *feel* Bhakti dasi has been extremely helpful.
   I *feel* my friend has been really nasty.

The significance is that the word "feel" isn't really expressing an actual feeling. It is assisting a thought, a perception. In empathic communication it is imperative to move away from ambiguous perceptions and transform those thoughts into actual feelings. We can be aware of our feelings, connect them to a need which will facilitate getting our needs met, and will in turn support becoming healthy and balanced individuals in Krishna consciousness.

An example of transforming thoughts into feelings:

   Thought:"I feel *stupid* when I sing."

   Actual expressed feelings:
   "I feel *sad* when I sing out of tune."
   "I feel *frustrated* when I sing out of tune."
   "I feel *uncomfortable* when I sing out of tune."

Expressing a thought without acknowledging the underlying feeling generates an assessment about the way:

> we *think* we are,
> we *think* others *think* we are,
> we *think* others are acting towards us or about us.

In order to avoid making judgments or perceiving others to be judging us (by hiding feelings behind thoughts), there is a need for clearly expressing our feelings. Be specific, whether you are assessing a current situation or something from the past; share the specific feeling.

The following words are often confused for feelings, but are actually words that label how *we think* others might be judging, perceiving, doing something *to* us, or not doing something *for* us

Cheated
Criticized
Exploited
Misused
Threatened
Coerced
Deceived
Harassed
Pushed
Victimized
Manipulative
Terrorized
Undervalued
Controlled
Disregarded

Exercise

See if you can determine which statements are *hidden* feelings, or feelings that are actually expressed:

1. "I feel you don't care."
2. "I'm frustrated that you are working after five."
3. "I feel sad that they are moving."
4. "I feel threatened!"
5. "You're being inconsiderate."
6. "I feel like speaking with her."
7. "I'm excited that you are coming for a visit."
8. "She is so unfortunate."
9. "When he doesn't communicate, I feel abandoned."
10. "I feel bad about what they did to him."

Answers:

1.HIDDEN – an actual feeling is not expressed and assumes someone's feeling

2.EXPRESSED – very specific, shares an actual feeling and why

3.EXPRESSED – "sad" tied to an observation of facts (moving) is a feeling

4.HIDDEN – "threatened" doesn't express how they actually feel; perception

5.HIDDEN – "inconsiderate" is labeling perceived action/motive of another

6.HIDDEN – "feel like" is not a specific feeling

7.EXPRESSED – a specific feeling is being shared

8.HIDDEN – not specific; there is not a feeling or observation included

9.HIDDEN – "abandoned" is a perception of another's motive, not a feeling

10.HIDDEN – "feel bad" is not a specific feeling, and no specific observation

Taking responsibility for our feelings requires:

> Evaluating our conditioning
> Getting to our core needs that produce our feelings
> Removing the layers of conditioning
> Revising how we give and receive

Explore transitioning from making generalized statements, to asking questions that will allow for identifying and actualizing real feelings. Here is a final example of the benefits of sharing empathically to identify feelings and core needs hidden behind a general statement.

> *Person A:*
> "My daughter never listens to me. I have no idea what to do with her!"

> *Person B:* (this response exemplifies the reverse of empathy)
> "I know exactly what you mean. My advice would be to pop her good if she won't listen, and when she does listen reward her with a nice treat. Then you won't have any problems at all!"

If Person B would take the time to listen instead of offering advice to Person A, Person A would have a greater sense of being understood by the opportunity to share, and relieved to be heard. For example:

> *Person B:*
> "Are you feeling anxious because you have a need to assist your children in reaching a higher level of Krishna consciousness?"

Person A would certainly feel more connected through this answer and empowered to explore their actual feelings about the situation.

When we use empathic communication to find our needs and fully express our feelings, and at the same time listen to others and offer them the same chance to fully express their feelings, then everyone's needs can be met. This allows us to have emotional freedom when giving and receiving empathically.

Emotional Freedom

When you learn the language of empathic communication, you will learn that no one has the power to 'make' you feel any particular way. This is emotional freedom. No matter what someone else does, no matter what name someone calls you, when you get in touch with your own feelings and needs, their words will no longer have "control over you." Actually, no one has *ever* had control over you, or *made* you do something, but because of unidentified feelings and needs that aren't expressed, it feels like an emotional prison. Empathic communication allows us to break out of this emotional prison.

Generally, three transformational stages take place when working to achieve emotional freedom.

1. Emotional Prisoner/Captive/Hostage Stage:

We think that we are responsible for others' feelings.

> We endeavor to keep everyone else satisfied.
> If they're not, we feel responsible and see those closest to us as burdens.

2. Belligerent/Rebellious Stage:

We feel angry and don't want to be responsible for other people's feelings.

> There is an awareness that, by taking on the responsibility of others' feelings, we're jeopardizing our own feelings.
> This awareness can bring about an *obnoxious* response. "I don't care about your feelings, I have feelings, too! Get lost."
> So, we're aware that we're not actually responsible for others feelings, but we haven't quite learned how to respond in an empathic way, reciprocating with others' feelings and needs.

3. Emotional Autonomy/Freedom/Choice Stage:

We begin taking personal responsibility.

> Our actions are stimulated by true compassion.
> We accept full responsibility for our own feelings and motives.

We allow others to take ownership of their own feelings and motives.
Our empathy is expressed clearly and we consider everyone's needs, including our own.

Hopefully you are starting to gain many new insights into your inner feelings. Throughout the day, stop and investigate how you actually feel. Then think about these feelings. In the next section we'll explore needs and how they stimulate these different feelings.

3rd Component: *Needs*

Empathic communication focuses on human needs. We assess whether these needs have been fulfilled or remain unfulfilled, then we work to rebuild the compassion and communication necessary for getting them fulfilled.

When we speak about needs in this context it should be understood that they are different than desires. Desires are strategies that may or may not be productive in meeting basic needs.

Our feelings come from and are deeply connected with these various needs. If we express our needs, we are more likely to get them fulfilled. Actually, everything we do is for a valid reason, and that reason is that we are attempting to fulfill our needs. In order to address our needs it is important to build a 'need vocabulary'. This will support our effort to identify when needs are being fulfilled and when they are not, as well as the feelings they ultimately generate.

The formula developed by Dr. Rosenberg for expressing ourselves empathically, is to connect a feeling to a need. "I feel __, because I need __."

Following are some of the basic core needs that everyone shares:

Basic bodily needs – air, water, food, etc.
Shelter – physical, mental, spiritual
Interconnectedness – reciprocation, giving, receiving
Self-satisfaction – self acceptance, autonomy, authenticity, acknowledgement
Spirituality – connection to Krishna, seeing others connected to Krishna, peacefulness

Realizing Our Empathic Nature

We all share basic needs, some realized and some unrealized. We each hold varying degrees of needs according to our nature. They are worth acknowledging and valuing within ourselves, and others.

As mentioned, feelings are representative of whether needs have been fulfilled or not. It's important to have a vocabulary of both types of needs and their related feelings, so that we can celebrate when a need has been met, or develop a plan for fulfilling a need that is not met. Following are two lists of possible feelings. Explore these, but also take the time to investigate and expand the list by making it personal.

General list of *feelings* when our needs are *fulfilled*:

Happy
Captivated
Blissful
Thoughtful
Overwhelmed
Passive
Wired
Enthralled
Peaceful
Pensive
Overawed
Calm
Pleased
Intrigued
Delighted
Engaged
Stunned
Moved
Joyful
Interested
Wonderful
Active
Dazed
Encouranged
Vivacious
Fascinated
Satisified
Preoccupied
Astonished
Confident
Ecstatic
Occupied
Content
Absorbed
Surprised
Assured
Thrilled

Attracted
Enamored
Focused
Impressed
Poised

General list of *feelings* when our needs are not *fulfilled*

Depressed
Fearful
Angry
Miserable
Afraid
Agitated
Unsettled
Anxious
Annoyed
Sad
Uneasy
Tense
Melancholy
Apprehensive
Stressed
Dismayed
Restless
Frustrated
Challenged
Frightened
Disturbed

There are a wide variety of words that can express feelings. By expanding our vocabulary, we are more likely to become aware of our internal motivations and gain the insight to make the necessary changes or plans to fulfill our needs.

Our Need for Autonomy

Autonomy is an interesting concept which is defined as "independence or freedom, as of the will or one's actions." Autonomy is one of the basic needs of the soul, the soul needs to be free to express itself.

The soul's autonomy is impossible outside of Krishna consciousness. Why is that? Krishna das Kaviraja Goswami explains this quite astutely in the Caitanya-caritamrta: "*Because a devotee of Lord Krsna is desireless, he is peaceful. Workers desire material enjoyment, jnanis desire liberation, and yogis desire material opulence; therefore, they are all lusty and cannot be peaceful.*"30

In other words, everybody except the pure devotee is controlled by cravings, whether those cravings are for gross enjoyment, for liberation or for powers in this world. The experience of cravings is not pleasant. It is an experience that agitates the mind and separates one from his original spiritual nature. When cravings become especially intense and one feels that they cannot live without the object of their desire, cravings are described as addictions.

We usually think of addictions as pertaining to some illegal drug habit, but addictions are far more widespread than that. There are food addictions (sugar, salt, fats, chocolate, etc). The proof that these are addictions is that we think we cannot live without them. We may have psychological and/or physiological withdrawal symptoms if we're denied these objects. One may be addicted to the experience of falling in love, adrenaline rushes (winning a competition), conquering an enemy, etc. One may even be addicted to the rush of enjoying the fruits of one's preaching (collecting money, disciples, and honors).

---

30 *Caitanya-caritamrta, Madhya 19.149*

Introspection is required to understand that we're suffering from these addictions. Why? Krishna explains this in the Bhagavad Gita. He teaches us that intense hankering, being addicted or having cravings comes from the mode of passion: *"The mode of passion is born of unlimited desires and longings, O son of Kunti, and because of this the embodied living entity is bound to material fruitive actions."*31

A pertinent fact concerning the mode of passion is that it gives one the illusion of the nectar of happiness in the beginning of achieving the object of our desires, but later that nectar turns out to be the misery that is equated with poison.

To fulfill our need for autonomy, freedom, there is a specific course of action prescribed for us. If we don't want to be autonomous then we can simply continue with our addictions. It is up to us. Cultivation of the mode of goodness will help us fulfill our need for autonomy.

In the beginning the cultivation of the mode of goodness may be a little painful, considering that we may still be experiencing some cravings. Gradually these cravings disappear and one experiences a great feeling of relief, nectar (Bg. 18.37). We can also understand from Bhagavad-gita that cravings are non-existent on the brahman platform, where one is qualified to transcend this world and perform pure devotional service (Bg. 18.54). Then the self can know true happiness.

I personally experienced this challenge when changing to my diet for health reasons. At first, the body's hankering after certain foods was quite challenging, but ultimately the bodily cravings disappeared. Now I experience relief. To be no longer controlled by cravings is like breathing fresh air or being let out of prison.

Spiritual freedom is much more blissful than being controlled by the forces of nature. In the spiritual world we'll get to fulfill our need for autonomy and experience it to the fullest extent. One may object to this statement and hold that the soul is never independent, and that even in the spiritual world we will be controlled (by *daiva prakriti* or *Yogamaya*), but

---

31 *Bhagavad Gita, 18.38*

the experience in the spiritual realm is that of voluntarily and ecstatically serving. There is no force.

In the Bhagavad Gita, Krishna does not threaten Arjuna, "Listen to me or I will send you to hell!" He does not use guilt trips: "You have been my friend for my whole life. I have given everything to you, Arjuna. How could you do this to me? You're killing me, Arjuna!" Krishna simply explains the facts of life, and then leaves it up to Arjuna to utilize his free will.

This is how we should offer Krishna consciousness to others. Here are the facts: 'Don't you want to be free? Don't you want to enjoy? Here is how. It is your choice.'

4th Component: *Requests*

When we make a request, it's to express what we need. When we request some action from people, it's most helpful if they feel they can trust that request. If we demand something from them they'll feel uncomfortable or unsafe and close down the avenue of communication. Demands will lead either to rebellion or submission. Neither one is positive or conducive to healthy relationships. For example, when someone says, "Don't do that!" most of the time we respond, at least internally, "I'm going to do just that!" You can't actually do a *don't*. It's not possible. A *don't* doesn't tell someone what you "do" want!

We are not able to force others to do, or not do something. With submission, someone may do something externally out of fear, but internally they will be rebelling. And with rebellion, one may retaliate and the other person may wish they had done that something – but still, the lack of desire to cooperate will not change.

Sometimes demands lead to violence, either physical or verbal.

Try to choose positive language all the time. When we request a specific action, we should indicate what we truly need. If we don't know what we want, if we don't know what we need, and if we don't express it clearly, it is impossible for others to understand. If we don't know, how can we expect others to know?

Requests, like feelings, are best expressed when they are specific and easy to understand; simple. Following are examples of requests, with the reason they are not likely to work.

Vague:."All I'm asking is that you be reasonable!"
What does "reasonable" mean exactly?

Abstract: "I need your help with the festival."
What "help" is specifically needed?

Unclear: "I just want to be treated fairly."
"Fairly" doesn't share specifically how someone is feeling, and what they might need.

You should know what you need. If you don't know what you want from yourself or others, it creates confusion. Confusion leaves needs unfulfilled and unfulfilled needs can lead to depression and anger. Anger may arise when people don't do what is demanded, or what is stated in an unclear fashion. It also comes from hiding our needs. Depression may come from ignoring our own needs, and doing things to be 'good'.

When and How to Make a Request

A request is made after we have expressed our needs, and it is the means by which we get our needs met. In the absence of a request, the other party will often think that they are responsible for *our* issue.

How we frame our request will have an impact on how it is received, and the response that follows. Leaving out the feelings and needs equals a demand. The way to avoid this is to say, "I feel . . . because I need . . Would you be willing to . ?"

Example:

Not an actual request: "I just need some help."
(Others might interpret this as, they *have* to do something in order to help out.)

Actual request: "I'm feeling really overwhelmed and need a couple of hours to organize the details of the festival. Would you be willing to call back later today around four-o'clock? I also might need your input to make sure everything is clear."

Request or Demand: How Do You Know?

The difference between a request and a demand can be easily detected by observing the person's reaction. If the person gets angry or upset, it was a demand. But when the person understands you and tries to see how you both can meet your needs, it was a request.

Observing the person's response will make clear whether it was shared as a request or a demand:

If they respond with a guilt trip or anger, they perceived a demand.
If they respond with understanding and cooperation, they perceived a request.
If they respond with criticism or a judgment, they perceived a demand.

Another tool that helps to clarify whether the other party has perceived a demand or a request is to ask the other party to *reflect bac*k what you said. Be sure to include an appreciation for their effort. Reflections usually come in the form of a question.

Example

"I want to make sure I shared my actual intentions and was wondering, if you would be willing to let me know what you heard me share?
"Wow, thanks for the feedback, it will really help me understand how I'm expressing my needs."

There is also the possibility that someone may not want to reflect back, being unsure of the intent or purpose of the request, in which case you can offer words of support and understanding.

Example

"What I'm hearing is that you would prefer not to reflect back what I shared. I would really like to be sure that you understand that my intention is not to test you about what I said, but to actually be clear about how I'm personally expressing my needs. Your feedback would be really valuable in helping me to understand."

When a response comes, we endeavor to continue in understanding the other person's feelings and needs. We also want to get a response that is clear and honest so that we can avoid any misunderstanding in the exchange. That means the best strategy is to ask very specific and clear questions.

Ask for feelings:

"Would you share how you're feeling about what I shared today? Also, if you would share   why you are feeling that way."

Ask for thoughts:

"I would like to hear your thoughts about my plan for the event, what works and what you   think might prove to be challenging?"

Ask for an action:

"Would you be willing to join me for the next planning committee meeting next Thursday?"

If someone responds in a way that doesn't provide what you are looking for, or if they heard something differently than what you actually intended to express, then try rephrasing the request. "Thank you for sharing what you heard. It's different than what I wanted to share and would like to try again to express my need."

The Complete Process of Empathic Communication Flow Chart

Observation + Feeling + Need + Requested Action

Next Page

Realizing Our Empathic Nature

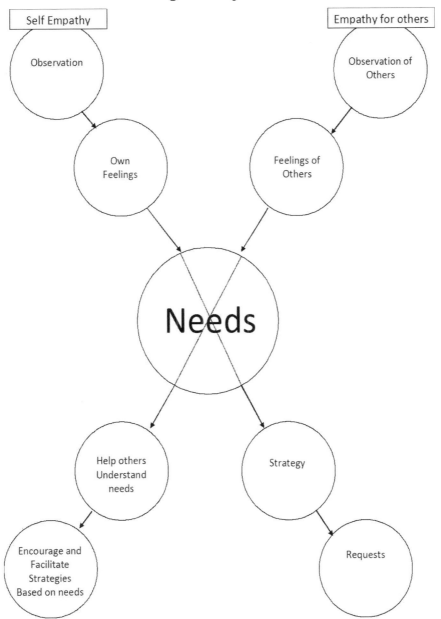

Self Empathy

Observation

Own Feelings

Empathy for others

Observation of Others

Feelings of Others

Needs

Help others Understand needs

Strategy

Encourage and Facilitate Strategies Based on needs

Requests

The Complete Flow Chart

In-Depth Review, Exercise & Additional Tools for Communicating Empathically

Observation *in Review*

Be very clear in your observation.
Use exact words spoken.
Use observable facts.
Avoid using generalizations.
Avoid using judgmental language that hides your thoughts, feelings or needs.
Avoid bringing in emotional evaluations that aren't based on facts.
Use the intelligence to filter out any criticisms, labels, or assumed intention of another.
Avoid using words like, *always*, *never*, and *seldom*, as they aren't specific observations.
Think about how others would possibly feel about the statements you might make.

Ask the question: Will the observation contribute to an empathic exchange?

Quick Exercise A:

Think of something someone does, one specific behavior that you don't like. Considering the points above write out the exact behavior as an observation. How clear (pure) of an observation, can you make?

Feelings *in Review*

One may not be comfortable being vulnerable because of the desire to protect oneself from being hurt. Therefore, we limit the number of words we use to describe feelings. But if we don't express feelings, it can make us sick. If we carry around unexpressed feelings, the emotional weight can actually cause physical illness. Feelings come from our heart, not from our mind. If we assume that thoughts are our feelings, we become disconnected from the real source of our emotions.

Remember to explore your actual feelings.
Use the lists of needs (fulfilled and unfulfilled) to help refine these feelings.
Start to utilize these expressed feelings to discover the underlying needs.

Quick Exercise B:

Imagine the person and their behavior from Exercise A above. Considering the points reviewed above and write down your feelings about the above observation. Write it out as, "When you did or said . . . I felt ..."

We have become accustomed to communicating in a judgmental way, but now we can take the empathic path of communicating from the heart. It will take practice.

Needs *in Review*

Being competent with empathic communication requires learning how to respond to others' needs with compassion. This is never about meeting our own needs at the expense of others, but about being responsive to our needs and feelings while empathically dealing with others.

Connecting with others is one of our main needs. When we judge others we are showing that we are focused solely on our own needs. We can try to guess others' needs instead of blaming them. We may be wrong in our guesses but the fact that we are interested in others needs will open up channels of communication. As soon as people begin to talk about what they need (rather than about what is wrong with this one or with that one) the possibility of finding creative and practical ways to meet everybody's needs is exponentially increased. It is essential that we teach ourselves to think and understand in the context of needs.

> Empathy involves being aware of others' needs and feelings, as well as our own.
> Become familiar with your core needs.
> Practice taking emotions and feelings back to the core need.

Remember that others are motivated by a core need as well. Also, review from the perspective of your new understanding

> What did someone do to stimulate these responses?
> How are blaming and judging expressions of unmet needs?
> Define the need behind the words.

Quick Exercise C:

Imagine once more you are dealing with the person from the previous two exercises. You've made an observation, identified the feeling, so now express the need. Use all the steps in expressing the need: Observation, Feeling, and Need (fulfilled or unfulfilled). You can try this multiple times.

Here is a complete example of the process from beginning to end:

> *"**When you said** yesterday that I should cook differently, **I felt** pain, pressure, and angry, because **I have a need** for autonomy and for making my own choices."*

Your greatest ally in this is *practice*. Then empathically communicating will be second nature for you. Love your mistakes. They'll teach you how to perfect the process.

Four Components: Exercise Review

I.   Distinguishing between *observations* and *evaluations*

Examine the following statements to determine whether an observation was expressed with or without a mixed-in evaluation. If an evaluation is mixed in with the observation, imaginatively restate the sentence so that only the observation remains.

> "My guru yelled at me yesterday for no reason at all."
> "Devi dasi watches a lot of television."
> "My guru is very generous."
> "That *sannyasi* weighs way too much."
> "The temple president complains when I talk to him."

"That *brahmacari* told me last night that he doesn't like my yellow sari."

II. Being able to tell *feelings* from other communication:

Examine the following statements to determine whether a feeling was expressed. If no feeling was expressed, imagine what the unsaid feeling might be and rewrite the sentence so that the feeling will be clearly expressed.

> "I feel that he is in Maya."
> "I feel discouraged."
> "When you act like that, I feel like leaving the room."
> "I feel rejected when my guru doesn't write me."
> "I feel abandoned by my friend."

III. Identifying our *needs* and taking *responsibility* for the related feelings

Examine the following statements to determine whether a need was expressed. If a need is not expressed, imagine what it might be and include it in the restated sentence.

> "I feel frustrated when you come late for class."
> "I feel happy that you won the prize for best book distributor."
> "I feel angry when you said that, because I want respect."
> "I feel scared when you yell."

IV. Expressing a *request* in present-positive-action language

Examine the following statements to determine whether the request was formulated in present-positive-action language. If not, restate the sentence to express it in that way.

> "I want you to understand me."
> "I would like you to have more confidence in yourself."
> "I would like you to stop drinking."
> "I would like you to drive at the speed limit or slower."
> "I want you to leave me alone."

Empathic communication requires presence, full attention, focus and space. It is ok for you to pause for a while, and not respond immediately. It requires intention as well. With EC, the desire should be to genuinely connect with a person and to help him or her, but not by attempting to fix any problems. We cherish another's pain by connecting on a deep level in order offer support, but we refrain from taking responsibility for removing it. Empathy is not fixing, but facilitating someone's effort to own the solution; empowering them. One of the greatest tools in empathic communication is observing. Not reacting. It allows time to gather, consider and reflect about a situation and how to create a win-win scenario by keeping empathy alive. This will contribute to our spiritual endeavors.

By utilizing the four components of empathic communication (observation, feelings, needs and requests) we ensure that our communication will be more effective.

Quick Overview:

Observation: State the facts.

> **"When you said, 'You boring old man.' . . ."**

Guess the feeling: Guess even if incorrectly, as it implies a desire to offer empathy.

> "When you said 'You boring old man,' **were you feeling angry . . .?"**

Guess the Need:

> "When you said 'You boring old man,' were you feeling angry **because you have a need for something exciting in your life?"**

Offer the Request:

> "When you said 'You boring old man,' were you feeling angry because you have a need for something exciting in your life? **Would you be willing to** attend someone else's seminar?"

Before we can respond in this way, it is essential to get in touch with our feelings and needs (which we'll explore later in the chapter in the section on *Loving Ourselves*). Otherwise, if we're not aware of what's going on inside our own self, it can block empathy, because there may be an initial tendency to get angry or feel emotional tension when we are being confronted by others. We can relieve this perceived mental pressure by being firmly in touch with our own feelings and needs.

Helpful Hints:

> To deal with our feelings it is beneficial to know the difference between *stimulus* and *cause*. The stimulus is someone's action that triggers a response in us. The actual cause is that our need is either being fulfilled or unfulfilled.

> If we are able to identify the need behind a feeling we experience, that awareness connects us internally. Knowing our own disposition allows us to be safe, even if vulnerable. When we are assessing our response, we may need some time-out before responding. Allow for it.

> Often when we are working empathically with someone we may start to feel our own emotions being stimulated and the desire to correct, educate, or perhaps advise. Then refocus the conversation and your intent back to being present for the other person. If your feelings are overwhelming or very strong, you can take the opportunity to internally practice self-empathy to again enable you to give the other person empathy and your presence.

> The error many people commit, especially in intimate relationships, is to think that all their needs are possible to be met by the other person. Often a husband and wife look to the other partner for their need fulfillment. After getting disappointed time and time again, both realize that their needs will not be met by the other person. This results in anger.

> There are many ways of meeting one's needs. The best practice is to avoid focusing on just one person or even a few to fulfill them. We should take personal responsibility to fulfill our needs.

> The reason self-empathy is so important is that without it we cannot give empathy to others. Remember, when we are not in

touch with the needs that are the source of our *own* feelings, we won't be able to get in touch with anybody else's feelings and needs, either.

How to Give and Receive Empathy

When connecting to others, we must listen for what others are *observing, feeling, needing, and requesting*. See behind their words. In this way, we can see their words in an empathic way; without judgment. Then we can reflect back to them what we understood was being shared, using the four elements. (observation, feelings, needs, requests). Reflecting back with those who might be upset, or angry, allows them to have the sense that we are with them (present), and gradually they will become more peaceful. Reflect back only if it contributes to greater empathy. In certain instances, the speaker may not need reflection, but we can still internally process empathically and reflect with our body language.

Often when offering empathy, you will transition through the following stages:

1. At first simply being present, and doing nothing else; just listening and observing.

2. Continuing to focus attention on another's feelings and needs.

3. Noticing any release of tension.

4. Reflecting back by guessing the other person's feelings and needs in the form of a question.

5. Asking for feedback.

How do we know when someone has received enough empathy?

Observing body language; usually there is a release or relaxed body language.

The flow of words being shared will usually become minimal or stop.

If you are unsure about it, just ask if there is anything else that needs to be shared.

89

It can be difficult to communicate with someone who says things that stimulate unpleasant feelings in us, and for us to work through the four components of empathic communication (observation, feelings, needs, and request), but it can be done. Remember, when someone says something unpleasant to us, we have four choices in responding. Two of them are out of touch with our heart and represent our customary ways of responding:

1. blaming the person, or
2. blaming ourselves

and two ways are empathic and in harmony with our heart:

3. loving the person, or
4. loving our self.

Our Choice to Respond

1. Blaming Others

This means finding fault with others. For example, if someone says, "You are *the* most self-centered person I've ever met!" We might react by saying, "*You're* the one that is totally self-centered!" If we defend our position and respond with anger or violence, needs are not expressed nor met, and conflicts will not be resolved. Putting the blame on someone else only abdicates our personal responsibility for our own feelings, and shifts it onto the other person. This is blaming the other person.

2. Blaming Ourselves

This involves taking things personally and hearing only blame and criticism. For example, if someone is angry and says, "You are the most self-centered person I've ever met!" We might choose to think, "Oh, I really *should have* been more sensitive." "It's all my fault." If we accept the other person's judgment and 'take on' the insult, it impacts our self-esteem and can lead to feelings of guilt, shame, depression, or anger.

3. Loving Others (empathy)

In practical terms, this means sensing another's feelings and needs. For example, if someone is angry and says: "You are the most self-centered person I've ever met!" We can respond, "Are you upset because you need your feelings to be considered?" Also, consider that in order to share empathy it may be necessary to first apply self-empathy (to avoid blaming oneself or the other person) before responding.

4. Loving Ourselves (self-empathy)

Here we sense our own feelings and needs by internally tuning-in to offer self-empathy, then respond according to our needs. For example, if someone is angry and says, "You are the most self-centered person I've ever met!" We can respond, "When you say that I am the most self-centered person you ever met, I feel upset because I really need my efforts to be recognized." This helps us to understand that we have needs and to express them, which can then provide the opportunity for getting those needs fulfilled. This does not always need to be expressed externally, although it can be.

Try to accept that the other person is not the problem. It is a matter of internal self-awareness and seeing that there are many ways and strategies for meeting needs.

Exploring Self-Empathy: Connecting to Ourselves

The tool of self-evaluation can help us move in a positive direction by offering respect and compassion to ourselves, instead of experiencing self-loathing, guilt, or shame. Shame is a form of self-hatred. It is crucial to learn to avoid the words or thoughts that include *should, must, have to,* because these oppose our strong need for autonomy and choice, and can cause us to lose our desire to contribute to life.

We free ourselves from self-judgments by recognizing our undesirable behavior as out of harmony with our needs. For example, we can pause and reflect, "I can see that I'm not acting in tune with my needs." "Why am I acting this way?" "So, what actually are my present needs?" Self-empathy lets us deal with emotional conditions and situations, to help us have a more balanced view, both internally as well as externally.

When we make a mistake, we should acknowledge it. Rather than becoming overwhelmed by the negative emotions of guilt, shame, or blaming others, we can mourn. Mourning is a way to connect with the needs that have not been met, and the feelings related to them, when we have been less than perfect. We use mourning as an opportunity to learn and move forward. Here are some valuable steps for revising our thinking around our mistakes:

- Hear and recognize the negative internal dialogue.
- See the needs behind that dialogue.
- Identify the feelings attached to the needs.
- Mobilize your creative possibilities for getting your needs met.

It is a big loss to be engrossed in self loathing. It disconnects us from our potential, from others and certainly from Krishna. We should use mistakes as opportunities to see our limitations and grow by transcending them.

Self-forgiveness is the follow up to mourning. In offering empathy to ourselves we're able to connect to our needs. The moment we make that connection, forgiveness takes place and gifts us with the choice to contribute to life.

Self-Empathy Exercises:

Transforming "have to . . ." *into* "choose to . . ."

Step 1

List on a sheet of paper everything you tell yourself you 'have to do'. Include in this, any activity you dread but do anyway because you 'have no choice'.

Step 2

Clearly acknowledge to yourself that you are doing these things because you 'choose to', *not* because I 'have to' do them. Insert "I choose . . ." in front of each item you listed.

Step 3

Complete the statement: "I choose to_____ because I need . _____ ." Work from your list of activities. This is to help frame the intention behind the choice.

Finding the intention behind our choice lets us continue the same activity, but with a very different energy. Now we can see its real benefit for ourselves and those close to us. We may need to repeatedly remind ourselves to refocus the mind on the purpose the action serves. This resets the conditioning and changes our consciousness related to the activities we previously disliked carrying out.

It's also helpful to be aware of the motivations connected to our choices and actions. We can, for instance, be motivated by…

> the desire for money (actually a strategy for meeting a need, not an actual need)
>
> the need for approval
>
> the hope to escape punishment
>
> the drive to avoid shame
>
> the possibility of avoiding guilt
>
> the sense of duty

Often, we are trained to strive for rewards, taught to be good to prevent not being liked or to avoid punishment, or to excel in order to receive approval. If language denies choice, it disconnects us from our core needs, fostering a robotic mentality that nullifies emotion and personal responsibility. This may be the most dangerous error of all. In contrast, it's most beneficial to have our choices stem from a desire to contribute positively to Krishna consciousness, not from fear, guilt, shame, duty or obligation. Consider that, even if we do serve out of duty or obligation, it is best to phrase it in our mind as a positive desire to please Krishna.

Assessing our actions and behavior through the lens of our unmet needs will provide a genuine impetus for contributing to our own and others' well being. Our greatest need is to eternally serve and love Krishna in an unlimited way. We can do this best by becoming Krishna conscious, loving all His parts and parcels, and compassionately bringing them to His lotus feet.

Love Yourself!

Contrary to the misconception that empathy just means loving others, self-empathy has the greatest impact on our own heart. We should naturally love ourselves because we are a soul, part and parcel of Krishna. If we desire to love Krishna, we have to love His parts and parcels, which includes us. So, empathy begins with ourselves.

Many devotees are under the false impression that they should love Krishna and denigrate themselves. It is understandable that they would think this way, because there are many easily misunderstood *shastric* recommendations such as *"thinking oneself lower than the straw in the street"*, *"the soul is one ten-thousandth the tip of the hair in size"*, *"the individual soul is tiny"*, *"one should be selfless"*, etc. We might also come in contact with people who, in the name of Krishna consciousness authority, denigrate us by saying we are "useless, hopeless, fallen, degraded, in maya, sense gratifiers," etc. In addition, we may be reminded about our past 'wonderful' (*vikarmic*) activities in this world, and that remembrance, will add to the negativity. This negativity may culminate in a lack of self-esteem and even self hatred, and from there lead to depression and deflate our enthusiasm to serve Krishna, We, may even think of ourselves as a "hopeless case".

I write about this subject matter because many devotees have talked to me about that mental state. When I hear devotees talk like that, it brings tears to my eyes, because I know that all devotees are very dear to Krishna. Even though ontologically we may be quite small, we are important to Krishna. We are not small in Krishna's eyes.

For example, we have the story of Gopa Kumar in Brihad Bhagavatamrita. Krishna had so much love for Gopa Kumar and hankered so much for his association in the spiritual world that Krishna Himself became Gopa Kumar's spiritual master. You may say that Gopa Kumar is a special devotee. In one sense, he is our role model. Krishna is personally the *Caitya Guru* of all of us, residing in our hearts and taking the trouble to direct us to our spiritual master.

Even before we took to Krishna consciousness, Krishna resided in our hearts, waiting for us to remember that our real happiness is in relating to

Him rather than to this external energy. Krishna considers us significant and important. When Gopa Kumar finally goes back to Krishnaloka, Krishna faints in ecstasy while receiving him. Even Krishna's associates hardly understood what was happening in that encounter. Krishna feels the same way about us.

What does it mean to love oneself? It means to picture, visualize, or imagine exactly how you want to be. Forget about all the negativity, whether it comes from yourself or from others. When you think negatively, that is what you meditate on, and those thoughts will impede your spiritual life. Acquire positive spiritual self-esteem! Do not remain in a situation where others are denigrating you! Reject arrangements that are unfavorable for Krishna consciousness and seek out favorable ones. You owe it to yourself and to Krishna.

Here are some things for you to think about:

> *"Radha and Krishna love me and want me to be with Them in the spiritual world!"

> *"Taking care of my spiritual needs cannot possibly impede my spiritual progress."

> *"Taking care of my material needs will not impede my spiritual progress either."

> *"I am an eternal spirit soul, full of bliss and knowledge!"

> *"I have an eternal relationship with Radha and Krishna and will realize this
> relationship."

Exploring Empathy: Connecting with Others

When we are empathically connecting to others, we give our full attention. We let them know that we are there for them. There are no ulterior motives, and we don't bring baggage with us. They may bring their emotional baggage, their anger, frustration, worry and sadness. However, by our connecting with them, they will eventually let go of their baggage and get to the real needs.

Realizing Our Empathic Nature

The major component of an empathic connection is just being there; presence. Presence means to be in the current moment, not in the past; focusing on what feelings and needs are present right now.

Components of connecting with others:

A. Presence – no judgment, no analysis
B. Focusing on and being aware of the other person's current needs and feelings
C. Offering confirmation of these needs if requested
D. Staying present with the person until the process is completed
E. Once the process is complete, reconfirming that with a request

We may assure the other person that we are there for them, and let them fully express themselves. Then we're able to get to the real needs – along with any present feelings, including their anger, frustration and sadness. Empathy is not intellectual understanding, theory, ideas, history, analysis or generalizations. It is appreciating the individual and connecting in the present.

You can "enjoy" their pain by connecting with them. (What you are actually enjoying is the connection and understanding you gain from the process.) When it is hardest to empathize, others actually need it the most.

When Working With Others

Move between empathy for others and empathy for yourself to make the process balanced and focused on communicating empathically.

- Practice self-empathy first.

- Being grounded internally you will be better able to offer empathy to someone else.

- Offer empathy, then do self-empathy again, followed by empathy for the other.

Avoid using pronouns like "it" and "that" as they really create a sense of impersonalism by being vague and lacking in personal accountability/expression.

- "*It* really makes me furious when there are mistakes in our flyers." (What "it"?!)

- "*That* irritates me a whole lot." (What "that" – action?)

Avoid statements that only emphasize the actions of others and don't include a need.

- "*When you don't* clean up I feel really hurt."

- "I get so disappointed *when you don't* include me."

Avoid expressing a feeling with the reason focused on the other person's action. Your feelings come from your needs met or unmet.

- "I feel (an emotion) . . . *because so and so* (other than me) is . . ."

- "I feel extremely hurt *because you* said that you don't care."

- "I feel so angry *because the supervisor* didn't follow through on...."

Remember to connect a feeling with the need: "I feel . . . because I need . . ." or "I wonder if they feel ... because they need ...."

Investigate

Guessing allows for clarifying and confirming:

- It helps to discover what someone really feels and needs.

- It allows you to be a facilitator.

- It allows you to become a reflecting agent so they can begin connecting to themselves.

Confirm (finalize)

Once they share their feelings and needs:

- Reflect back what you have heard.

    - Reflecting back continues the connection.

    - It helps you to gain greater understanding and depth.

    - It helps them to see themselves.

    - It lets them appreciate your efforts.

Exercise

If someone says: "I am really depressed," how would you respond?

Remember:

- Don't confuse empathy with sympathy.

- Sympathy is self-focused; empathy is focused on the other person.

- If you find yourself connecting to your own emotions and feelings, do some self-empathy so you can refocus on finding the other person's need.

- Inquire with no expectations or personal motivation Request an opportunity to connect with the other person so you can be gifted to receive and share empathy.

- Avoid trying to fix, correct, give advice, or offer a generic "I understand."

- Ask the other person to share any sense of criticism as you work through the situation
  - This allows them to feel safe to express their feelings which is challenging enough
  - It also allows for you to understand how you are expressing yourself and how others may interpret that expression

See no evil in people. Everyone is simply looking for the best way to get their needs met. Remember everyone, all the time, is only working towards the best way to get their needs met, however they may express it.

Keeping Empathy Active

Demonstrate understanding rather than just saying it in words by continuing to…

- focus and be present in the current moment, not on the past, but on the *immediate* need

- help draw the other person away from the past to again focus on the current feelings. What is the need right now?

This can be challenging when somebody is going on and on without actually touching on any feeling or need, It can be hard to follow exactly what they want. When someone keeps talking, wandering all over the place, they are usually not aware of their own need, and try to find it externally through dialogue. If you connect empathically to the present, it can help others do the same. Then needs can be met, and there is closure and understanding for everyone.

How you might respond:

1. "Excuse me." (You can interrupt.)
2. "I'm having a hard time following you."
3. "I want to make sure I really understand."
4. "Are you feeling . . . because you need . . .?"

Empathy Without Words

What about showing empathy to someone who doesn't respond at all? Is it possible to connect with someone who doesn't say anything? Yes, absolutely. All it takes is staying present. Guess their feelings or needs and be fine with the silence; let it be a tool.

Spoken words mean very little, as most people interpret through body language rather than words. If you say something and your body language says something different, what the person will perceive is the body language. Words only make up 8% (some say 12%) of communication. Words are not the person. And behind every philosophical position that people have taken, there's a psychological mindset. *If you go only by the words, you'll never understand the meaning.*

Sharing an Empathic No

Avoid sharing an outright *no*, because when you say *no* it can stimulate anger. The most practical way to share *no* to a demand is to realize that by making a demand, the person is revealing his or her mind in regard to their needs. We endeavor to perceive it through their eyes (point of view), and see it as a mind-revealing gift. If we're not able to do this immediately, it may be necessary to share our own feelings and needs first, and then we can make a request to express the *no* empathically.

Examples:

1. "When you asked me for money I felt anxiety because I have a need for security and peace. Would you be willing to discuss other ways to achieve your needs?"

    or

2. "When you asked me for money, did you feel anxious because you have a need to support your family? Would you be willing to talk with me about alternatives?"

If you don't make a request from the beginning, it is most likely to be perceived as *no*, or as just some big excuse, and you may be perceived as being very selfish, which is actually only due to your unexpressed need. So, in this case the request is actually meant to get both your and their needs met.

With empathy, you're not obliged to come up with a solution, but you are obliged to communicate with the other person. It's necessary to demonstrate interest in another person's needs when sharing your perspective. Your sincere interest will help them discover various strategies to meet those needs. So, your commitment is only to communicate.

What About No?

Why are we afraid to say no? There are many reasons for not expressing no. We may fear that someone will not understand our underlying need, or that they may respond with an emotion that is uncomfortable. The problem is that 'no' doesn't fully express the underlying need. At the same time, it disconnects us from the opportunity to allow the other person to express their needs, which is why there is often a 'negative' response. Although apparently negative, remember it is an unfulfilled need being expressed, and you can help find the root *feeling* and *need* that is generating the response.

Remember:

- If someone makes a request, even a demand, show through your body language that you have received an opportunity to connect.
- Even if you do want to say no, AVOID IT. *No* does not express the need and disconnects us empathically. Be sure to express your need. Tell them why you're unable to say yes.
- End with a request that seeks to meet everyone's need. It is important to think about *no*. Why do others say it? Why may you be afraid to say it? There's always a need behind a *no*.

How Can Anger Be Controlled?

You can control anger by practicing forgiveness. How do you forgive someone who has apparently done something to you? First, you see Krishna behind it. Next, you see that they are suffering, because when they do something out of anger or for some other reason, they're the ones actually suffering. If you're the one who is angry, remember your anger hurts you, not the other person. Through empathy you can see that an angry person is suffering, and you can feel compassion for them because you understand the source of their anger.

Why do we have uncontrolled anger when our true Krishna conscious nature is to always be compassionate and connected? According to Srila Rupa Goswami, the Krishna conscious devotee does not feel anger. When needs are not being met, that is what stimulates anger, either in us or another person. By finding out which needs aren't being met in any given situation, you'll come up with a strategy for meeting the needs.

Once the needs have been addressed, there will no longer be any impetus towards anger. It's imperative to learn what to do with anger, which brings us back to distinguishing stimulus from cause. It is the cause we want to focus on and recognize (the underlying need), whether it be a judgment or a diagnosis. Then state, "I am angry because I need . . ."

Being angry is not wrong. See anger in a positive way. It is a sign that you have unfulfilled needs. Anger is like the warning light on your automobile dashboard. The light is not the problem. The light simply indicates another deeper problem

However, anger is not productive in getting your needs met.

Exercise:

Try to remember the last time you were angry.

1. Write down the stimulus (that triggered the anger).
2. Then write down the cause (the unmet need or value).

Take the opportunity to explore your needs every time you feel angry or any other feeling that is not contributing to your life or core values in a way you would choose. This constant practice will support you and provide invaluable tools as you progress on your devotional path.

Four Steps in Dealing with Anger

1. Take time to stop, breathe and reflect before responding.

2. Recognize any judgmental thoughts (towards yourself or others) you may be carrying.

3. Ascertain any needs that are not being fulfilled.

4. Express the feeling and the underlying need that is not being fulfilled.

• Stop • Reflect • Assess • Express

Anger is something less than desirable. It is one of the *anarthas* (unwanted things), which are impediments to achieving the goal of Krishna consciousness. There are many verses about controlling anger in the *sastras*. The question is, however, how we should deal with anger, especially the kind that comes up when we have been insulted.

We generally adopt the tactics of suppressing or repressing it. Suppression means that we are aware of being angry but are concealing the symptoms. Repression means that we push the anger down and deny altogether that we have an issue. Neither suppression nor repression is a healthy way of handling anger.

Suppressed or repressed anger will sooner or later resurface in some other context, either directed toward another target or towards ourselves. Repressed or suppressed anger can also take a toll on the physical body. One can develop ailments like bruxism (grinding down one's teeth during sleep). Internalized anger is known to cause organ damage. Bodily difficulties or syndromes, and even serious diseases such as cancer are typically related with emotions with which we have not come to terms with. We certainly want to respond to insults in a healthy, Krishna conscious way.

What are healthy ways of dealing with insults?

One of them I refer to as the *Jada Bharata method*. Jada Bharata, who had previously been Bharata Maharaja – and for some time had taken birth as a deer – was insulted by a king while he helped carry the king's palanquin. Jada Bharata, out of compassion, jumped to avoid some ants in his path. When the king hurled insults at Jada Bharata, he responded by explaining that all the king's insults were in relation to the body, and that in actuality we are not our body. So, this method of dealing with stimuli works by being unattached to the body, which renders body-based insults completely ineffective and thus not worthy of attention.

Another one is the *Haridas Thakura or compassion method*. Haridas Thakura was being whipped in many market places and yet could only feel overwhelming compassion toward his tormentors. Being impervious to the brutal whippings, Haridas Thakura would hardly have wasted the energy to take notice of insults.

A third one is the *Dharma the Bull attitude*. What makes this method truly potent is the acceptance of every circumstance as a beneficial arrangement directly made by the Supreme Personality of Godhead. Therefore, all that needs to be done regarding insults is to discern what the Lord has chosen to teach through them, learn from it, and then act appropriately.

The fourth is the *Token Reaction method*. It appreciates every negative experience as a token reaction to one's past misdeeds. One understands that if they keep serving Krishna enthusiastically with body, mind and speech, they will be a fit recipient of Krishna's mercy.

> *"A devotee in a calamitous condition treats it as a benediction of the Supreme Lord and takes responsibility for his past actions. Faced with such a trivial thing as insults, he merely offers more devotional service and remains undisturbed. With such a disposition and engagement in devotional service, they are the most eligible candidate for promotion to the spiritual world, whose claim on promotion to the spiritual world is assured in all circumstances."*32

---

32 *Srimad Bhagavatam, 10.14.8*

The *fifth way* is suited to those of us who have not completely realized our spiritual nature yet. Here one experiences the anger without suppressing or repressing it and identifies what unfulfilled need is at the root of it. One views the insults or other external events simply as a stimulus rather than the basis for the anger. By being in touch empathically with the self, one recognizes the unfulfilled need as being important, not the external occurrence of insults.

In order to be materially and spiritually healthy, we must deal with our emotions in healthy ways. When we are disconnected from our needs we become angry; but if we connect with them we will experience empathy. A benefit of empathic communication is to be able to transform anger into productive thinking, feeling and behavior. Instead of suppressing or repressing anger, we get in touch with it by observing our feelings and needs. We do not blame others for our anger, because we value taking responsibility for our own feelings and needs.

Why Be Aware of Your Anger?

Because it is the key for unlocking those feelings with which we need to deal. Treating anger with awareness can also reveal other emotions and thus more needs. It can be an effective tool for bringing many of our needs to the surface so that we can actually get them fulfilled. If we avoid being aware of our needs our spiritual advancement can be hindered.

Anger perpetuates itself through "enemy images." It is important to understand this, and to work to eradicate these enemy images from our heart. It is part of the material disease and hinders devotional progress. Try to understand that every criticism or judgment is simply a distorted manifestation of an unmet need. This not only applies to our anger, but others' anger as well.

Whenever someone stimulates our anger, it will most likely be necessary to get in touch with our own feelings and needs first, as this will enable us to truly extend empathy towards that person. The same may be true when our actions stimulate anger in others. It's an opportunity in either situation to help discover the underlying needs so that we can work to get them fulfilled. This will make us stronger for future challenges, while enabling the practice of forgiveness to help us foster empathic relationships within the Krishna conscious movement.

Observation is a critical key to objective awareness. Try to analyze as if you are a spectator, not personally (emotionally) involved. For example, someone makes a statement while being apparently angry or critical; notice how you feel. How is your body reacting? What is your mind thinking? Review what they said. Does it resonate? What is Krishna trying to share? Go over the scenario again, and try to understand what might have stimulated their reaction. What could you do differently? Are you okay internally with your actions that stimulated theirs? Check for personal values and needs, as well as feelings. And finally try to become familiar with and utilize the different methods shared above.

CHAPTER FOUR

Raising Children Empathically in Krishna Consciousness

Srila Prabhupada placed a great deal of emphasis on taking care of the younger generation. In the beginning days of the movement he took some money from the BBT to establish the *gurukula*. That original *gurukula* was in Dallas, Texas. Later, Prabhupada also put a major portion of funds from the BBT and other resources into the school in Vrindavana. Nurturing children in Krishna consciousness was an extremely high priority for him. If we examine religions around the world to see what binds a religious community together regardless of which faith we are examining, we will invariably find it is emphasis on caring for children.

Voluntary Spirit of Devotion

For those who do not have children it is difficult to understand how much attention children require while they are being brought up. It takes more effort than Deity worship. At least Krishna (the Deity) goes to sleep at regulated times, He eats at regulated times, and He takes His bath at regulated times. Krishna is rather well behaved, but children are not exactly regulated. They take up approximately 80-90 percent of their parents' time. Thus, when children are not engaged in Krishna consciousness it means parents' attention is also diverted from Krishna consciousness. For instance, when parents send their children to different types of schools, they will become more and more attentive to what is going on with their children's schooling in a non-Krishna conscious way rather than a Krishna conscious way. They generally spend time driving their children to soccer games, or this game, or that game, whatever it is, but their attention is directed away from Krishna consciousness.

Can We Awaken the Voluntary Spirit of Devotion in Children?

I know that in many areas there are no Krishna conscious schools, so in this chapter I will attempt to suggest ways of encouraging children to take up Krishna consciousness. You cannot force a child, or anyone else to be

Krishna conscious. It has to come from their heart, their own desire, and their own free will.

We have a need for autonomy, for making our own decisions in life. Children also have a need for autonomy. They are persons, individuals, and spirit souls. We often misinterpret their intentions and think that they behave terribly. They are only expressing their need for having a separate identity. The more we try to force them to be Krishna conscious, the less Krishna conscious they will be. Children respond to force in two different ways: they can either rebel, which they do most of the time, or they can submit. If they submit, they will not be acting from their heart. They obey simply to avoid punishment or to obtain a tempting reward.

I heard of a temple that posted the rule that if you did not go to *mangala arati* you had to fast for the entire day. Some devotees who were subjected to rule revolted and left the Krishna consciousness movement. Even had they outwardly gone to *mangala arati*, would they have actually been in attendance? Srila Prabhupada said that we are where our mind is, not where our physical body is. When you do something voluntarily your heart and body act together. When you do something involuntarily, under the threat of punishment or lured by a promise of some extrinsic reward, there is an internal disconnect. Prabhupada said that when we are raising children we have the responsibility of instilling that voluntary, enthusiastic spirit of participation of Krishna consciousness.

Interacting with children empathically is not a technique but a consciousness. It is worth learning to do. The same dynamic applies to working with adults in a hierarchical situation. I will not share a technique. Instead, I will share a consciousness. Techniques are mechanical patterns, while real life situations are unpredictable, dynamic and changeable.

Consciousness is more important than any technique. When techniques are used on others, they may perceive that we are trying to manipulate them, that we are not being honest with them. Eventually they will no longer believe or trust us.

In management, there is a technique called the "one minute manager." Applied in a Krishna conscious scenario, for example it means, that if my disciple does something incorrectly, I have to first praise him for one minute ("You are such a good, fantastic devotee. What would I do without you?") In the next step, I would chastise him for a minute ("But you did a lame job translating today. Better have your wife do it next time.") And the third step would require me to praise him again ("Anyway, you really are a sincere devotee, wonderful, ecstatic, so dedicated, and such a talented cook too.")

That is how we apply techniques. So, the next time I see him, and make a nice comment about him, he will think, "What is coming next?" Therefore, we are not interested in techniques, but we are interested in the proper attitude, in consciousness, connecting with others, connecting with children, connecting with our friends, connecting with adults, and ultimately connecting with Krsna. So, if you are reading this chapter because you want to find out how to control your children and make them behave nicely – or maybe you want to learn how to control your wife or your husband to make her or him behave nicely – you are reading the wrong book.

External Behavior

When I ask the parents at my seminars what they all would like to see their children become in the future (when they grow up), they often come up with a list like: fulfilled, happy, Krishna conscious, balanced, responsible, mentally and physically healthy, filled with love, independently thoughtful, wise, honest, compassionate, respectful (from the heart) to elders, hard working, loyal, creative, and so on.

In this chapter I will point out how the traditional methods we currently use for dealing with children (or disciples, or people working with us) do not help us achieve our goals, and I will teach you a methodology that does facilitate the attainment of these goals.

When we interact with children or with people who work under us as our subordinates, we generally tend to turn to control. Control means that we are largely interested in what is termed external behavior. A child is described as good when that child is quiet. A disciple is considered good when they don't talk back to the guru and just says, "Yes, sir!" But when we say, in everyday language, that someone is a "yes man" it is considered an insult, isn't it? Do we really want children to be that way? Do we want "yes children?" No, but we act as if we did want them to be that way.

Imagine that you are a child, and I want you to do something for me and say, "I want you to translate for me, and if you won't translate for me I'm going to spank you." Could you imagine me acting like this with an adult? Suppose that a married man treated his wife like that. What if the husband says, "Listen to me real good or else I will beat you." In most countries, one would call the police and report that man for abuse. Why do we accept it when someone does it to a child? It is interesting, isn't it? I would never accept it. Why should we allow doing this to a child, who is helpless and emotionally vulnerable?

Example

Controlling the Child's External Behavior

Let's see how children react if they are being dominated over. Say, for example, that I'm a father yelling at my son, "Go to your room!" And if he won't do it, I'll turn up the volume of my voice. "Better go to your room *NOW* or I will hit you!" How will the child respond? He just wants to be himself and do things voluntarily, like adults and every living entity. Will my child obey me, coming from his heart, after an exchange like the following conversation?

Father: "I want you to go to your room, boy!"

Son: "I don't want to go to my room."

Father: "You heard me! I'm your father."

Son: "It doesn't matter to me that you're my father."

Father (raising his voice): "You're supposed to obey your father. And I am your father. Do you want to get spanked? Go to your room!"

Son (scared): "I don't wanna go to my room."

Father (yelling): "Then you're gonna get it! You won't be able to sit for a week! Just go to your room right now!"

Son (sniffling and in a low voice): "I don't wanna go to my room."

Father (amiably): "That's alright, *(moves hand threateningly and yells again)* but you have to go anyway!"

Finally, the child does go to his room. But let's review what has happened in this particular example. The child is not going with his heart, he is going resentfully. As soon as I turn my back, he will come out, draw on the walls with crayons, throw everything around, create a disturbance; and now his relationship with me is no longer full of love, trust and cooperation. He will feel alienated from me, his father. It ruins the relationship, destroys trust, and creates havoc in his life. In other words, nothing beneficial can come out of this type of dynamic called punishment.

The Harmful Effects of Control

Throughout many academic studies conducted with parents who tried to over-control their children, parents will focus on using a controlling behavior instead of making a connection with their children. This type of autocratic environment generally makes people sick in different ways. It can be manifest in physical sickness and/or mental sickness.

A study of 4,100 adolescents showed that as teenagers with authoritarian parents they were obedient and comfortable, but had very low self-reliance, and social and academic abilities.

Another study concluded that children have a good capacity for self-regulation. That means they will know when they are hungry, how much they should eat and when to stop eating. But, children whose parents forced them to eat at meal time when they weren't hungry, did not want to eat or finish their plates, and lost the ability to regulate their eating habits later in life.

When I was young, my mother would try to make me finish everything on my plate. Of course, it was not prasadam, and when I refused she would take the food and throw it on my head. Heavy! Now today after 60 years I'm not actually able to eat the type food that she used to force me to eat (especially beets)! My mother also used to say (it was after World War Two) "You must eat everything on your plate, because people are starving in Europe!" Of course, I was not submissive and just said to her, "Send it to them!"

Studies show that over-controlling parents can undermine a child's moral development. This means that the children are unable to think and reach decisions when they have an ethical dilemma. They have less resistance to temptation when they are offered intoxicants or drugs by their friends, and show evidence of less conscience. Do you know what a psychopath is? It is someone who has no conscience and no feeling about anything.

Another study shows that children of over-controlling parents are less motivated later in life, feel worse about themselves, and don't internalize their own sense of values and morals. A modern-day advocate of using control techniques on children and for dealing with people in general, is the renowned psychologist B. F. Skinner. He is a very interesting personality, who conducted many animal experiments and then wrote books about people based on his studies. For legal reasons, he could not experiment on people. But evidence-based research proves that the methods people use for controlling external behavior have exactly the opposite effect. People who use them get the reverse effect than they desired.

Heavy behavior control of children can have one of two results. You can get a robot with low self-esteem, or a child who is extremely rebellious. A child also learns the art of dealing with other people from his parents. For instance, if parents generally say to a child, "You better listen to me or I'm gonna whip you!" guess how that child will treat children younger than themselves, or people weaker than them?

We have seen this dynamic unfold in our movement, between the temple president and the mid-level manager devotees under him, or between a spiritual master and his disciples. The mid-level managers treat devotees under them in the same way the temple president treats them, and a disciple treats devotees whom he instructs in the same way they have been treated by the guru.

When I joined the movement, *sannyasis* were not nearly as kind and gentle as they are now. They often treated subordinates in a very heavy way.

Example

There is a tendency to deal with our children as our parents dealt with us.

You can review the below scenario, and then role-play it with the same or a more relevant situation in your own experience. One devotee can take the role of the child and another devotee can take the role of the adult and imitate their own childhood experiences.

Child is crying.

Mother: "Why are you crying so loud? All the neighbors can hear you. What's wrong with you?"

Child keeps crying

Mother: "Don't cry! What will the neighbors think of me?"

Child keeps crying.

Mother: "Don't cry! Only weak people cry!"

Child keeps crying.

Mother (annoyed): "You won't accomplish anything in your life if you cry all the time!   What's the matter?"

Child (crying): "I won't tell you because you're yelling at me."

Mother (yelling): "I'm not yelling! Tell me what's wrong! What did you do?"

Child (crying): "Mom, something bad has happened to me."

Mother (yelling even more loudly): "O, my God! What have you done? What?"

Child (crying): "Promise you won't punish me."

Mother: "That depends on what you've done."

Child (crying): "Promise . . ."

Can you imagine how the child felt? When she heard that, did she want to stop crying? Not really. Of course, it is very traumatic for children when their parents attempt control them through force. And, if they become submissive they will lose their ability to control themselves. They will become dependent upon external control.

Example

When a Child is Forced to Eat

If a child is forced to eat when they're not hungry or has to eat preparations they don't like, they may develop eating disorders later on in life. What this force-eating does to children psychologically is to make them lose their ability to know when they are eating too much as adults. It is a major cause of adult overeating because there is a loss of the internal control mechanism. In the next scenario, a son revolts against his father who is forcing him to eat a preparation he does not like.

Father: "Finish your pumpkin!"

Child: "It tastes bad."

Father: "That doesn't matter. It's been offered to Krishna."

Child: "Maybe He doesn't like it either."

Father: "It's prasadam. Don't disrespect prasadam. The pumpkin was offered to Radha-Syamasundar. You have to eat it!"

Child: "I don't like it."

Father: "Open your mouth and put your spoon in it! You aren't getting up from your seat until you finish it. Do it!"

Child: "And, if I don't?"

Father: "If you don't, you're gonna spend the rest of this week in your room!"

Child: "With the pumpkin or without the pumpkin?"

Children know what and how much to eat. That does not mean we give them a choice to have a thousand lollypops. We put healthy food in front of them and they know when they are or aren't hungry. They know how much to eat, so we do not need to force them. Children have a natural ability to distinguish this need in their own bodies. My brother was also forced to eat. Our mother used to stuff food into his mouth to make sure he ate everything on his plate. But right afterwards he would go to the bathroom and just spit it all out into the toilet.

A university study showed that children two to four years old, who were forced to eat, lost the ability later to discern how much to eat. As mentioned earlier, when you force children to behave in a particular way they lose the ability to internally distinguish or judge what is ethical or unethical. External factors will override their internal judgment in the future. So later in life, when they are with their friends who may have bad habits, they won't be able to say no or to judge for themselves.

Example

A child who was not able to say no at the crucial moment:

There is a "good" little boy who was nicely trained by his parents. In other words, he always had to do what he was told. Let's see what happens when he meets one of his friends who is smoking marijuana.

Friend: "Take some!"

Boy: "Er . . ."

Friend: "It's good for you! Don't worry about it. Everyone does it! Don't you want to be one   of us, enjoying with us?"

Boy: "Hum .."

Friend: "Try it! It's good! Come on!"

Boy: "But, my parents . . ."

Friend: "Your parents will never find out anyway. Don't be a sissy! Take it!"

Boy: "Oh uh alright alright just for you, buddy alright "

Why Do Children Lie?

Children may lie out of fear when they are accustomed to excessive discipline. So, they'll figure out a way to lie and hide the truth from their parents. They are no longer revealing their minds to them. They don't have a trusting relationship with their parents. They may also become sneaky in their behavior.

Punishment Paradigm

On one side there is, "If you do this, then this will happen to you." Then there is the flip side, "If you don't do this, then you won't get this or that." These tactics equate to or shape behavior by either causing the child suffering, or by threatening to cause suffering. In this way, temporary compliance is forced but no conscious change happens, nor does the child's discriminatory faculty improve. In fact, it begins to atrophy (break down).

Suppose that somebody threatens you with a gun and says, "Do what I demand or I'll shoot you!" It works. It's actually a very effective strategy – for the short term. We should always use it, right? The question is though, why should parents have to quit using it, if it is so effective for the objectives of controlling and manipulating behavior? Think about that! The challenge of the punishment paradigm is that in order to be effective it has to be continued, or else it will stop working.

Many studies have proven that this authoritarian type of manipulative behavior used by parents stands in an inverse correlation with that child's healthy behavior later on in life. In other words, there is a direct correlation between this kind of domination, and subsequent disruptive behavior. This not simply my opinion; studies have established this as fact. And, it's valid across all socio-economic strata. The studies show that this type of punishment ethic promotes aggression, depression, and a desire to exert control over others in the future.

Different Types of Punishment & Their Effect

Time-out

There is a handy little punishment that parents like to use called time-out, which seems to be a very nice method of disciplining children. Have you ever heard, "Go to your room. I don't want to see you for the next two hours"? What children are thinking when they hear this is, "My parents

119

are rejecting me." They see it as a withdrawal of love. This method erodes the relationship between parents and children. Children eventually begin to see their parents as enemies and no longer as their friends.

Police-like Parents

How do you feel when the police are driving right behind you? Do you think, "Oh how nice, they've come to protect me, "They must really love me," or do you feel threatened that they are going to pull you over for a traffic infraction? In America, we have a gadget called a police detector. It is an electronic device that can detect the radar signal of police cars five kilometers (3 miles) ahead. As soon as it goes "bip, bip, bip", you slow down, fasten your seat belt and put on your best behavior.

What do you think about the idea of children feeling this way about their parents? When they hear the parents coming they think, "Red alert! The police are coming!" or when disciples hear the guru's footsteps, they say, "Oh not again! It's the police!" We don't want that. It will not be productive in forming compassionate human relationships and loving connections between people.

Averting Punishment

Another problem with the punishment paradigm is that it tends to distract one from the most important issues. Rather than learning positive behavior, the focus will be on navigating past the looming, lurking obstacles of punishments.

Imagine for a moment that I am a child that is hitting my little brother. How would I ever learn that this is wrong when my attention is on how to avoid getting caught red-handed by my parents? Studies show that a child's sound moral development requires an absence of punishment. Isn't that interesting?

When we get punished, we learn that 'we' are bad, but we don't learn that the 'activity' is not good. Why shouldn't I hit my little brother? What is the reason? Can you think of a good reason for why it's not a good thing to hit him? The actual reason is that he'll feel pain. If you say, "It is bad to hit him," it does not mean anything to me as a child. All I hear is, "You are bad for hitting him, and you'll get punished for it." I will be unable to develop empathy for my brother, and I won't learn that the logical reason for not hitting him is that it causes him pain. Since I know that I don't like to feel pain, I would naturally not want to create pain for others. It's simple and just takes some effort to explain it in terms the child understands, and will help the child develop empathy. "Oh wow! My little brother feels pain whenever I hit him on the head. That's awful! I'll never do that again to my little brother."

If you wish to change someone's behavior, ask yourselves two questions:

1. Exactly *what behavior* do I want the person to change?

2. What do I want to *explain as the reasons* for making this change?

Reward and Punishment:

Two Sides of the Same Coin Called Control

Previously I mentioned an example given by Marshall Rosenberg in his book *Non-violent Communication:* He was at an airport once, and saw a mother and child. The child was amazingly quiet and never cried. He asked the mother, "How are you doing this? How do you get the child to be so quiet?" The mother said, "I have a philosophy. I give him either a cracker or a smacker." Her philosophy was to train a child the way circus animals get trained. If you've ever seen a trained dolphin jump in and out of the water, you noticed that every time he jumped they gave him a fish. Do we really want children to be like that? I do not think so. On the other hand, we do not want to be overly permissive parents either, who just let children do anything they would like to do. If we are in touch with the children's needs and are able to communicate with them about their needs and our needs, children will more easily understand what is the best course of action.

For instance, if I want my child to do something and say to him, "Go to your room! If you go to your room, I'll give you a piece of chocolate cake, and then we'll go to Disneyland where you'll get ice cream too," he'll most probably go to his room right away, and I fulfilled my desire as well. At the same time, there is no relationship. He is not interested in working with me, or having a relationship with me, or being respectful to me. All he's thinking about is chocolate cake, not in helping me meet the need I have for him to go to his room and clean. My need is the last thing on his mind, and the relationship isn't communicated as being important.

Parents tend to stick with the same soulless manipulation when children go to school. We tell them, "If you do well in school, you'll get that video game you want!" I remember when I was young I'd get money for every A I brought home, but if I did not get an A, then I was not my mother's son! She used to tell people, "My son would never get anything but an A." Can you imagine how traumatic that was? It may not sound so traumatic, but it happened to me over 50 years ago, and yet it is still painful for me to remember. Think about it! Getting money for every A did not encourage me to like studying. It encouraged me to focus on money instead of the personal relationship.

Stanford University studied two-year-old children playing with blocks. It was obvious that the children really enjoyed playing and were having a great time. But, when their parents started to reward them for playing nicely, the children lost all interest in the blocks when their parents were not around any longer. The researchers concluded that the more you reward somebody with extrinsic things (meaning that the reward has nothing to do with the activity itself), the less interested in the activity a person will be, even though they were interested in it beforehand.

I enjoy giving seminars because they facilitate my preaching Krishna consciousness, but let's see hypothetically what would happen if I would get paid a ten thousand euros/dollars for every seminar I would conduct. Even though I can presently give seminars from six in the morning until ten at night, I could lose interest in them if they turned into a paid performance. I could lose interest in helping people through my seminars. That same thing happens to children too.

Reward & Punishment Place Emphasis on the False Ego

Knowing all this, we can safely assume that rewarding children as a means for shaping their behavior produces the same effects as punishment. It steers them toward becoming self-centered and liking the rewards rather than the activities for which they're being rewarded.

So, instead of thinking, "I really like accomplishing this," the child will think, "What's the most I can get for doing it?" In this way, both reward and punishment put the focus on the child instead of others and encourages them to be more self-centered. Their main concern will be whether something will get them rewarded or punished. They won't be thinking of other people's benefit at all or the joy from doing a particular activity.

Why Parents Favor Using Control Methods

What is so attractive about disciplining, controlling, rewarding and punishing children? Why are we still doing these things despite having heard about all the statistics?

The reason is that they are easier and take less time. They also facilitate our needs rather than the children's needs. When you can say, "Do this or I will hit you!" or, "Do that and I will give you something you like," you will not have to bother explaining to children how their acts will cause someone else pain. It is an easy, quick way to accomplish our purpose.

The problem is this way you will convey the message to the child that in the real world you have to learn how to overpower people if you don't want them to do "bad things" to you or you will have to bribe people to get them to do something for you

We may also want to vicariously enjoy through our children, pushing them to do something that will entertain or please us, rather than thinking about their lives.

Example

When I was young my mother told me, "You should become a doctor!" I asked, "Why?" She said, "To please me." I asked, "Why?" She said, "Because I am your mother." Even now she keeps telling me that I should leave spiritual life and go to medical school to become a doctor (at 67 years of age). If I did that I would have to specialize in geriatrics!

Her mantra is, "Make me proud of you!" Often we are pushing children to succeed for our benefit. We can see this with sports. Parents will insist, for instance, that their children be number one in football or some other sport.

We even preach to our children, "If you don't obey me, the Yamadutas will come to get you! If you are not a good devotee you will go to hell!"

Another reason parents use controlling methods is that they've heard from many others that this is the way to deal with kids. There are many books on raising children, and some of them state, "Spare the rod and spoil the child." You can't get much more absurd than that. Also we believe children are lazy, rude, irresponsible, or like animals; or we believe that punishment and reward will get the child's attention right away.

Many parents have an internal need for validation, to prove to themselves that what their parents did to them was "right." It can be hard to admit that one's parents were wrong. We want to believe that our parents did what was best for us. These are some of the many reasons we deal with children as we do.

How to Be Compassionate with Children

The empathic-supportive method disdains punishment or reward. It shares empathy, reasoning, human warmth and love. Parents frequently subscribe to a false dichotomy, holding that you must be either excessively permissive or excessively controlling. They do not see that this is a black and white conception bereft of the natural shades of gray in between. So, I suggest a third path of interacting with children that requires neither dominating nor bribing them nor being permissive.

Example

Uncovering and validating the child's needs

Father: "How are you doing? How do you feel today?"

Son: "I'm fine, thanks, and you?"

Father: "I'm alright too. I'd like to talk with you about something that we could do   tomorrow. How about we take a trip somewhere out in nature? Later we could do some hiking. Would you like doing that together?"

Son: "No, not really. Could we fly a kite instead of hiking, what do you think?"

Father: "Of course we could. If there's enough wind tomorrow, why not? It would be a lot of fun for us, I'm sure."

Son (excited): "Wow! I can't wait to try out my new kite!"

Father: "I know a great place where we could do that. But to go there we'd really want to start early, so you'll have a lot of time for flying your kite. That means going to bed early. Does that sound good to you, going to bed early, getting up early, and then – let the games begin?"

Son: "Sure, dad. I think going to bed early is a cool idea!"

Father: "That's settled then. You wanna help me get your kite to the car?"

Of course, it's not always so simple. But, the method stays the same. I'm presenting my needs, ask for his suggestions, and continue being empathic with his needs and what he likes to do.

With school, it might be a little harder. In connection with school you could lay out the reasons, and ask, "What do you think you want to do in the future?" It will be a little bit more complicated, obviously, maybe a lot more complicated. Still, you empathize with his needs and clearly reveal your own needs.

The important thing is to change our strategy from doing things *to* children to working *with* them. When we work with children they develop a sense of individuality and learn to make their own decisions. They are being educated to think for themselves. You say, "Why should I want my children to think for themselves? I just want them to be obedient." But, the problem with their being obedient is that in fifteen years, they may wind up being obedient to a gang instead of to you. As we see from the role play in the example of being offered marijuana, a child will sooner or later run into someone at school who says, "Smoke this!" "Come with me and do this. It doesn't matter what your parents think!" The child will not have the sense of discrimination and the mental strength to say no at that point, because you trained him in blind obedience.

Unfortunately, I have also seen this play out in our movement, with devotees who have been trained the same way. They form different groups, have group leaders, one group thinks they're better than the other group. People follow the leader rather than thinking for themselves. This affects the unity of our movement.

In Germany, you had the Nazi group in which most people followed the leader blindly, without discrimination.

People can snap into this consciousness, the herd or gang consciousness, because they have lost their individual sense of discrimination. Do we want our children to be like that? As an organization we need to have the goal of creating a better world for our children.

Example

What we go through as children exerts a strong influence on our whole life

A seminar participant took the part of a child in a role-play, and the other person played the role of his father who tries to send him to his room, first by threatening him, then by using the empathic method. The devotee playing the role of the child shared his experience in the following way.

"When I played the role of a child it immediately took me back to childhood. I remembered my father who punished me for everything. As soon as my role-play partner raised his voice and said, "Go to your room!" I felt pain in my heart. And then, when he was trying to send me to my room in a gentle and nice way I suddenly remembered my mother who with affection and tolerance explained the reasons for doing things. I have three children now and I always try to give them love and tell them patiently what is better for them."

We could see that he went through some intense emotions during this exercise. This devotee was in his mid-thirties at the time of the seminar. What happens in our childhood has a strong influence on our whole life. It is good to remember that the way we deal with our children will have a lifelong effect on them.

Ten Principles of Raising Children Empathically

At the beginning of this chapter we established that raising children empathically is not a technique but a matter of consciousness. It's a consciousness filled with compassion toward another living being that is momentarily inside a smaller body than ours, and has physical and mental capabilities that differ from ours, but is the same kind of spirit soul as we are, with full rights to be heard and respected. We showed why control methods do not work in dealing with children and showed an alternative way of interacting with them, the empathic or supportive method.

Understanding that control methods do not work in the long run and that we, as parents (gurus, leaders, senior devotees) cannot achieve our long-term goals by using them, it's important to inquire what it means to put the supportive method into practice. How can we, in a real-life setting, demonstrate our compassion for the child and others who are subordinate to us, through our words and actions?

On the following pages, I'll present ten principles of empathically interacting with children, and with those in a subordinate position. These principles also apply to any type of relationship, including dealings between adults. In this chapter, we will concentrate for the most part on children.

Applying these principles in your everyday life will bring you closer to your children, and you'll be able to communicate with them in ways that do not harm or cause them trauma. This entails avoiding the four D's of miscommunication that we discussed in chapter two, namely, diagnosis, demand, deserve and denial. You will be able to connect to your children and every living entity through empathy. Part of this is willingness to be vulnerable, and at the same time being aware of the child's feelings and underlying needs.

If you adapt the model outlined below to your specific situation, you'll have a better chance of raising a happy Krishna conscious, balanced and healthy child.

1. Consider Your Request

Before asking children to do what you want, it's important to take the time to rethink the value or necessity of the request. If the child does not respond favorably to your request, it is probably due to what or how it was being requested. An unfavorable response is a very distinct indication to rethink the strategy being used. Try reflecting. Think it through until you feel clear about what you will say or do, before you say or do it.

Consider your request. When it involves a child, it is most beneficial to keep your eyes on the long-term goals. How do you envision your relationship with your child in ten or twenty years from now?

It requires a dose of humility to admit that we were, or are wrong – especially if you have a stereotyped concept of your position as a parent, guru or sannyasi, etc. It is often hard to say, "I have made a mistake," especially for a guru who is universally expected to be absolutely perfect, and powerful. I have done this, gone to disciples and shared, "I have made a mistake. Please forgive me. I am far from perfect, but I will try my best."

It will probably come as a surprise when you discover that adults and children respect you more for your vulnerability. It is more pleasant to be a human being than to be perfect. The highest praise anyone can give or receive, at least from my perspective, is that one is human, in the sense of naturally endowed with strengths and weaknesses. It beats being called "perfect" hands down, anytime. I value being thought of as a human, a real person.

One reason for the dissatisfaction or unhappiness to which people in high positions often seem to be prone, is that they tend to act out of tune with their personhood. People should act naturally. I am not suggesting that a sannyasi should "let down his hair" but it will not diminish their stature to be normal, a *mensch*, as they call it in Yiddish.

So, rethink your request if you find it necessary. Appearances notwithstanding, it is not at all certain that the unfavorable response was the child's fault, or that they did not want to do what you asked.

2. Put the Relationship First

Make your relationship with the child your first priority – before anything else. What is more important to you? To be right or to have a close, loving relationship with your child? What is the most important thing to you?

Recognizing the answer to this crucial question may sometimes require you to take a time out. You should not inflict the dreaded "time out" on the child. *You* take the time out, and rethink your request. If you ever feel yourself succumbing to anger, take a time out. It's a good idea, because anything you say will be influenced by anger, and it will definitely stimulate a reaction.

This, by the way, goes for e-mails too. If you feel angry while communicating with someone by e-mail, do yourself a huge favor by not pushing the send button right away. Go to sleep, look at it the next day, and then decide whether you want to send it or erase it. I think it was Abraham Lincoln who counseled, regarding letters written in an irritated state, "Put the letter in your drawer, and you will most probably rip it up the next day."

When you act from anger and hate you will stimulate another person's distress. This is a red flag! You may think, "The kid should shut his mouth," but actually the healthiest response is to refrain from reacting at this point, take time out to think about it, consider what you actually desire for the child. Reflect on how you envision them becoming in the future and how this will impact that outcome, the long-term goal. This is an important determination.

We do have needs for another person. For example: I have a need for you to be happy. That is a bona fide need. Within relationships we're likely to have needs for others. I don't need you to obey me. That's not a need but a strategy, as defined in empathic communication language. But we can have needs for other people's needs. I have an actual need for you to be happy. I have a need for you to be protected, to be self-fulfilled, to be healthy. These are all needs.

Human needs encompass the needs for others. Therefore, instead of pressuring children or the people who work with you to do something, work on a caring attitude of facilitating with them. Before making a request of a child or someone, rethink it. What is more important to you, the request or the relationship? How do you want the child, disciple, vaisnava to develop? The loving relationship is more important than the behavioral compliance you desire.

When a child is crying, your first priority should be your relationship with the child. Try to understand which of child's needs is being expressed.

Being right is not important. Again, equip yourself for admitting to your child or disciple that you've made a mistake if you have.

I was with a *sannyasi* once who said, "I don't make mistakes. I made just one mistake in my whole life. It was thinking I had made a mistake." Of course, he was joking. People admire the someone who's able to admit having done something wrong, whereas a person attached to the notion that they cannot err is liable to lose others' respect. Be vulnerable. If you make a mistake while dealing with your child, just share "I am sorry. Connecting with you, and understanding you, is definitely the most important thing for me."

3. Love Is Unconditional

Don't withdraw love from a child – for any reason! Let me give you an example from my own childhood. My mother would often say that *my* son only gets A's." She had, no doubt, unconditional love for me – I know my mother pretty well – but as a child I only heard, "You are not my son," and painfully felt it as a rejection. All over something trivial like a school grade. Now I have to confess that I went out and I bought invisible ink. Then I turned the B into an A. I learned to do it, and when I showed the report card to my mother she would sign it, suspecting nothing. Later the ink became invisible, and that A turned back into a B again. So, you see, I had to earn her love, by hook or by crook.

Love is indispensible in our relationships. You will make mistakes and children will make mistakes too. That's all. You can be proud of your child if they do something well, and just as proud if they do something not so well. If they make a mistake you can say, "I am proud of you. It's encouraging to see you trying your best." Like your love, your pride as a parent is most valuable if it's unconditional. If you praise a child for only doing the things that you want, it will create nothing more than insecurity.

So, whether you're a parent or a superior, make your love unconditional. Suggest to your child or subordinate, "I love you for who you are, not for what you do." This is a very important point. Regardless of what they do or don't do, you love them. Prabhupada was like that. Often a disciple would leave the movement or get caught in some nonsense activities, but whenever they came back, Prabhupada would be nothing but happy!

College students participating in a study were asked whether their parents loved them more when they showed good behavior instead of bad behavior. Close to eighty percent of the students answered, "Yes, my parents love me more when I act in a way they like." Next, the parents were asked, "Do you always love your children, no matter what they do?" These parents uniformly said, "Yes." They didn't realize that they had not expressed unconditional love to their children.

It all boils down to how children perceive their parent's words and behavior. It's vital that your child has no difficulty perceiving and experiencing your unconditional love. You don't have to like everything they do, but be sure it doesn't obscure your love for the child. Be extremely cautious of sending out the unintended message that you no longer love them.

Many studies back this up. Studies indicate that students who perceived that their parents loved them only conditionally are at greater risk of disliking their parents.

This is especially true with teenagers They may acquire patterns of self-loathing. It may come from the experience and perception of having love withheld. Avoid facilitating this perception. It is not what you *think* you're doing that's at fault but how the child perceives and interprets it. You may think to yourself, "I didn't mean it like that," but that doesn't work when you deal with a child. It is essential to learn to clearly communicate with a child.

It takes awareness when interacting with children so they *feel* unconditionally loved instead of assuming it's enough that *you* know you love them. We love our children, but it takes a conscious effort to get them to *feel* loved. Instead of thinking in your mind, "How can I get my child to do what I say," ask yourself "What does my child need, and what kind of communication and actions will help me, as a facilitator, to meet these needs?"

Let's be clear that "needs" aren't equivalent to superficial wishes or impulses. Fundamental needs are connected with Krishna. Needs are also connected with our survival and functioning in this world. Think, "My child has a need to be connected with Krishna, as well as other needs. I am choosing to be aware, present, and attentive."

4. Imagine How Things Look from the Child's Perspective

Put yourself in the child's shoes. In my seminars, we use exercises and role playing to see and feel what it's like being a child. The different physical appearances of an adult and a child shapes their different views of reality. Between adults this difference may be subtle, existential, as in the different perspectives which characterize the hierarchical positions and philosophical levels within a society.

From your child's point of view, you may appear as an overpowering and sometimes frightening giant. In one exercise, we have the adult stand on a chair and the adult acting like a child crawl on the ground. In this way adults, can vividly experience the differences in power and stature between a child and adult. The child looks up to a giant, and see him/her like Hidimba in the Mahabharata.

Imagine that there was someone bigger than you, a giant. Your head just reaches up to his knees. His head is practically touching the ceiling. He is thundering at you. "Go to your room or I will spank you." How would it make you feel?

Putting yourself into someone else's shoes or switching roles is a good way to resolve almost any conflict and develop close relationships. As humans, we all have needs and emotions.

5. Be Authentic

Being yourself, a human being, a regular person, will create the environment for reconsidering your request, admitting that you made a mistake, or taking the risk of making a mistake that exposes your vulnerability. These things can only be done from the heart, not by following a system. It's a matter of caring and focusing on sharing options with your child that in the long run will build a strong relationship and help the child be aware of his/her own needs.

"I want you to be happy, fulfilled, and healthy." These are needs. "It's not about what you'll choose as a profession when you grow up." Some old friends of mine forced their children to be doctors. The child says, "I do not want to be a doctor," but the parents insist, "You *will* be a doctor for us.

6. Talk Less, Listen More.

Talk less and listen more; ask more. This can be a hard one, but God has given us one mouth and two ears. We should listen twice as much as we talk! Listen to what the children say. Ask them to share from their particular perspective, and if they cannot talk, try to guess empathically how they see things or how they feel. Ask them, "How do you feel about this? What do you think, is there a different way this could be done?"

Take the example of your wanting the child to clean up his room. On the one hand, you're thinking that you need cleanliness because you don't want a bunch of cockroaches running around, and on the other, you're thinking about connecting, having a personal relationship. You talk to him about it. "Why do you think it is important to have a clean room?" You discuss this with him, back and forth, and let him talk, contribute. Let him explore the different perspectives. "If you were me, what would you be thinking or feeling?"

Of course, he might sometimes say, "A kid has a dirty room." He'll challenge you like that. But you simply keep on going back and forth for a few days. It takes longer to deal with children empathically, but it's an investment that has profound impact.

Realizing Our Empathic Nature

A demand rather than a request takes no time and is easy, "You'll do this or else!" Threatening to spank or actually spanking a child may be quick, but it's a shortcut to dysfunction.

You can have family conferences about different things. (I'll explain this in more detail in point ten.) Let the child participate in the family conference as a full voting member. Ask, for example, "What do you think about going to the Krishna camp?" instead of just dictating, "We are going to the Krishna camp!" Because if you dictate, the predictable answer may be, "I don't wanna go." And if you insist with, "That doesn't matter. I am your mother. We *are* going, whether you like it or not!" the child will not be a happy camper when you do go.

7. Ascribe the Best Possible Motive to the Child

Have the understanding that the children have a good motive. In other words, do not think, "those little rascals, those idiots, those demons, they're just trying to harass me." That is not what they are thinking at all. They are just trying to meet their own basic needs.

Say, a child is crying. You might think, "That child is crying just to drive me crazy." But the reason children cry is not to drive people crazy. Children cry because they want food, they need their diaper changed, they are in pain – there is a reason why children cry, a valid reason, their needs that should be met. Children are not busy plotting how to make your life miserable.

The worst imaginable motive we can assign to a child is that they are crying to drive us crazy or they are simply playing a game called "manipulating mom." Isn't it true that we oftentimes ascribe the most fiendish motives to children? They are just crying to communicate a need. We say, "Oh, the kid just wants attention." But what is wrong with a child wanting attention? They need love and have already figured out that love doesn't come without attention. So why do we imagine it as such a negative thing? "They are just looking for attention!" Have you ever heard this? He or she is a child. A child has the desire for love. Attention is a strategy to obtain the love that the child needs. Everyone has the need for loving exchanges. Rupa Goswami acknowledges that in the Upadesamrta. Giving prasadam, accepting prasadam, giving gifts, accepting gifts, revealing one's mind in confidence, hearing from others, are all parts of loving exchanges. Why would a child not have that common need?

There is a particular stage in a child's development that usually occurs when the child is two years hold. The parents sometimes call that stage "the terrible 2s." It is simply the stage in which the children are trying to establish themselves as individuals, a completely normal phase in a child's growth and normal expression of the child's need.

The worst punishment that my mother inflicted on me was what she called "cold shower." It meant that she ignored me, did not look at me, and did not talk with me. I was a non-entity. I was a ghost. I said, "Mom, are you there?" but she just continued ignoring me, and that drove me crazy. I felt that I was no longer important to her.

In every case, it is advisable to attribute the best possible intentions, consistent with the facts, to the child. Even if children lie, there is likely a motive that is not altogether negative. They're scared. They're trying to protect themselves. Why do children lie? Out of fear, and the need to protect themselves.

8. Try to Say Yes Whenever You Can

A technique often used by parents is called 'the automatic no' response. Whatever the child might ask, the reply is automatically no. "Can I do this?" "No." "Can I go here?" "No." "Why?" "Because I said so." Have you ever experienced that? This shows a fundamental disrespect for the child as a person. And that is how the child interprets it, because while they are being outwardly dealt with in conversation, no consideration is being given to what the child is actually experiencing internally. So endeavor to avoid unnecessarily saying "*no*." Think about it twice or three or ten times before you say no! We are prone to using this *no* that automatically springs from our mouth if a child asks us for something. Before you say *no*, first consider, then explain your feelings and needs behind that *no*.

Let's apply this to two adults. When a disciple says to me, "Gurudeva, I would like to go to Disneyland today. Let's go to Disneyland!" and I reply, "No! That is maya!" it would not stimulate a positive response or feeling. But if I answer, "I am experiencing so much anxiety because I have all the responsibility Prabhupada gave me. Could you ask someone else to go with you instead of me?" It would be then easier for them to understand my need, isn't it? If you flatly say *no*, it practically amounts to denying the relationship. What the other person will hear is a "you're an idiot," which is an insult, ie they are in maya. These perceptions come from one unexplained *no*. They will a different impression, a positive impression if I explain it in such a way that it is clear that I am taking responsibility for myself, by explaining what I feel, what my needs are, and requesting that they choose another strategy.

9. Utilize Flexibility

Try to avoid being too rigid with children. Although a regulated lifestyle really *is* preferable, everyone needs a little flexibility. It is not a good idea to demand that children do the exact same things, at the exact same time every time. We often impose unbending rules such as the children's bed time. "This is your bed time! You have to be in bed by eight!" Sometimes cut them a little slack. If they're excited and want to stay up a little later, don't bark, "You MUST be asleep by eight!" Talk with them about it to see what they think would be beneficial, and agree to make a little adjustment in their daily program, as a special exception.

10. Let the Kids Make Decisions Whenever Possible

Give the children more chances to make decisions in the family. When you are planning your family vacation, sit down with your whole family and let the children be part of the discussion. Imagine how things look from the child's point of view. When you're thinking of going to the beach for example, instead of just telling them that you will all go to the beach, make request for a family meeting, and ask for everyone's input. This is called an *istagoshti*. An *istagoshti* is an interactive participatory meeting amongst devotees. It's a forum for entertaining different ideas, and every devotee gets a chance to participate. When you let children enter into this type of interactive process, it will help them become independent thinkers and problem-solvers. It trains them to make intelligent decisions, instead of depending on being told how to think. This will protect them from the negative peer influence that we mentioned earlier. It will also reduce their risk of getting involved with things that aren't supportive of a healthy and joyful lifestyle, or habits that could cause harm to them. Peer-group pressure should not be underestimated. It can have a devastating influence on a child's capacity for self-determination. You can use this *istagoshti* process even if the children are just one- or two-years-old with a limited ability to speak.

Bring the children into the decision-making process and validate their need for autonomy. Research shows that teenagers who participate in the family decisions are more likely to stay out of trouble. They see themselves as a part of the family. They don't feel alienated as dominated children do. Obviously, the child should not become the leader of the family. They do get to share their opinions, but these may still be overruled when others' opinions are better matches for everybody's needs.

Things to Remember When Applying the Ten Principles

These are some principles for dealing with children empathically. To succeed, try to imagine how you would feel, and how you would want to be dealt with if you were a child. Doing this, you can realize how best to act and what would be best thing to say. It's not as important to understand what the child thinks as it is to understand how he/she feel and what the needs are. Your child will appreciate your efforts to understand even if your guess as to the child's feeling and needs is not correct.

Remember the child's age and interact with the child in ways appropriate for that age, because at different ages children will have different capacities for comprehending and expressing ideas.

Take your time and avoid rushing while communicating, otherwise your interactions may be unpleasant for you and the child, and you won't have a favorable outcome.

Questions and Answers Regarding the Raising of Children

Q: I decided not to punish, but what shall I do if the child rejects fulfilling his obligation?

A: Give me an example.

Q: For example, my son sometimes rejects fulfilling his obligations for school and does not do his homework. And sometimes he neglects his room. Then how can I persuade him?

A: It is a process and takes some time. It is not very easy. We should try to invoke empathy for our own needs on the part of the children and show empathy for their needs. If we do not do that, the children will not do as well in school as they could. They will develop distaste for going to school and for cleaning their room, which I did.

Studies show that empathy evokes desirable behavior, what to speak of the connection. But it takes more time and more attention than control methods.

My mother forced me to clean my room. After I cleaned it, she would conduct an inspection. It was like being in the army. She would make sure that the bed had what she called "hospital corners." When the bed didn't look perfect she ripped off the covers, threw everything on the floor and made me do it again. When she was present I did clean my room but whenever she was not there I would deliberately take everything in the room and throw it all over the place. I really enjoyed doing this! Then I would even go into their room (she'd told me to never enter it), where she kept expensive antique couches, and jump on them like a trampoline.

Had my mother sat with me for a long enough time to explain, "If you clean your room and make your bed, then you will succeed in life, and you will become a good bed-maker, and people will like you more." I might have developed an attraction for doing it. Just sit down with the child and explain things in terms of the child's own interests how it will help him fulfill his needs in life. Here is a little role-play to illustrate this.

Father: "What do you want to be when you grow up?"

Son: "A pilot."

Father: "A pilot? Wow! That's wonderful! Do you want to fly big planes?"

Son: "Yes."

Father: "Wow! Let's talk about how you can do that. Pilots are all really great at mathematics. Why? Because they have to calculate the distance between different places, and they get to look at all those little screens. Isn't that cool? And then they control different things with the sticks, and they also learn how to speak English so that they can call the control tower and say, "Flight 32 coming in for landing!" So, they need to learn good English and mathematics. And geography too, because if they are going to India, and they end up in Africa instead, that is a big problem."

This was an explanation made dealing with the child's desires and needs. He would most likely be more inclined to study. Becoming a pilot is *his* goal in life, not mine. I have a friend who was forced to be a doctor by his parents, and as soon as he became a doctor he said, "I did this for you, but now I'm gonna do what I want to do," He'd spent eight years in school! Let children live their own dream.

Q: Isn't that manipulation?

A: No, because being a pilot is *his own* desire. I am just explaining to him *how to achieve* it. I am facilitating his desire.

Q: But there are also children who get punished a lot, and due to their suffering developed empathy for other living beings.

A: That may happen. What you say is actually true. But the majority of people who suffer a lot (because of excessive punishment) when they are children, deal with subordinates in the way that they learned from their parents. So it is not that the majority of people who are punished learned, "Oh, I have to be empathic and not treat people the same way." You are correct. Some of them do. Most of them do not.

How to React when the Child Does Something Beneficial

Q: How to praise the children in the right way? For example, if they made nice puppets.

A: I would not give some general praise. I would say something like this, "You have painted the puppets very nicely. I feel happy seeing them." Basically, express happiness and your need. "I see that you are becoming creative." In this way you express appreciation, not just general praise. Show how much you appreciate and love the child in all circumstances. They should get the message, "I love you because you are you. I love you not because of what you do but because of who you are."

It's vital to express our love for them regardless of what they do or do not do. This increases the child's sense of security. When a child comes back from school, you can say, "I am really happy to see you." Not because they were on time or got an A. Just, I am happy to see you. How many times do we give that unconditional love to anyone? Between husband and wife, or between friends, or between spiritual master and disciple, love is sometimes expressed if someone did something, not because of genuine affection.

There is a difference between praise and appreciation. Praise is very general, which really does not help someone. Like, "You are so good." "You are so wonderful." "You are fantastic." This does not help someone. But when you see something that someone does and you express *specific* appreciation for that *particular* activity – that will not inflate the false ego and will encourage the person. Prabhupada did this. Someone held a *Ratha yatra*, and Prabhupada wrote, "I heard about your Ratha yatra. I was happy to hear about it. Please go on and on doing this to fulfill my desire that I had for many years."

> He wrote in a letter to Upendra, *"Your strong desire to serve me is very beautiful. You are serving me and I am serving Krishna. I am also a servant so I cannot accept service from you."* Here Prabhupada expresses appreciation in a very Krsna conscious way.
>
> To Jayananada, *"I am feeling very intensely your separation. In 1967 you joined me in San Francisco. You were the first man to give me some contribution for printing my Bhagavad*

Gita. After that you rendered very favourable services to Krsna in different ways."

This is in a letter to Bhakta das in San Diego. "I thank you very much for installing Radha Giridhari. From my childhood, I was very fond of Radha Krsna. My good disciples are helping me to open many Krsna temples all over the world."

So Prabhupada was expressing very specific appreciation for what somebody did. He is expressing his heart, his own needs and feelings, his connection with Krishna. And it certainly did not puff up anybody. It just encouraged people to follow Prabhupada more. He was very expert in giving appreciation.

Q: But what if even appreciation makes my daughter proud and then she goes to her friend and says, "You do not do it nicely, I do it nicely" or something like that?

A: Then you can to talk to her and explain, "Your friend also did nicely. But you are my daughter and I love you very much. Whatever you do, I love you." The important thing is to express unconditional acceptance and love. Not for what they do, but for themselves.

Q: What is the line between rewarding children and making them conscious of their needs?

A: There are two words in connection with this, "extrinsic" and "intrinsic." Extrinsic rewarding means getting rewarded for an activity with something that has nothing to do with the activity. It is given to manipulate the the person. Intrinsic rewarding means that the activity itself and the enjoyment of performing it is rewarding.

Let's look at an example. My mother might say, "Go to school and I will give you 5 dollars." That is an *extrinsic* reward, which does not connect me with the activity of going to school. It connects me with money. If I like money, so I'll do what is necessary to get money. However, if my mother had said, "If you go to school you will learn about music. It really is fun," she would have been connecting with my need and offered an intrinsic reward. In another context, this type of reward is called the *natural consequence* of an activity. Pointing out to a child the natural consequence of the activity is not manipulation. It's helping the child be enthusiastic about the activity in tune with the child's needs.

Parents sometimes use food to reward or punish the child. "If you're good, you will get plenty of sweets to eat." "If you're bad you won't get anything to eat at all." What will happen when the child learns to equate food with appreciation and love? What will they do when they get older? They will eat when they are not hungry to fulfill their need for love and appreciation. Thus they might gain an unhealthy amount of weight. It is a common problem.

Q: *What could we do in a positive way if our children have done something wrong? I have heard there is a village somewhere where if someone does something wrong the elders praise them.*

A: This is part of the process called restorative justice. Love is expressed for the person. As Jesus Christ says, "Hate the sin but not the sinner." It is utilized help the person understand how his or her acts have affected other people or themselves. Condemning someone does not work. The Bible contains another instruction, "Judge not lest ye be judged." Another quote is, "Let him who is without sin throw the first stone." There are many statements in the Bible about loving, forgiving, and not judging.

For the children, love should always be unconditional. That means loving them whether they are "good" or "bad". You can express appreciation for something that they do, and you can help them understand how they would hurt other people or not meet their needs, if they carried out a certain action. You can clearly communicate to the child "I love *you* because *you* are *you*." That is all. If the right attitude is there, then the right words will manifest. It is not a technique.

How Can I Involve a Small Child in Decision-Making?

Q: *You have mentioned that we should make decisions together with the child. But what about a two-year-old child? You cannot rationalize things with them.*

A: I would not tell the child what to do. Empathize with him or her, and express your own feelings and needs. After the age of two, the need for autonomy becomes more pronounced. That is why people often refer to that age period as "the terrible 2s." But they are not really terrible. They're actually quite wonderful, these terrible two's. The child is beginning to express himself or herself as an autonomous individual, independent from you. Parents should appreciate that. The child is saying, "I am an individual. I am no longer part of your body. I can now differentiate myself from you." We can appreciate the child for communicating that. It is the natural way of unfolding the child's individual potential.

When children are accepted into the decision-making process, it allows them to develop the ability to solve problems. It encourages them to become independent thinkers, and to learn how to play an active role in deliberating, negotiating, and planning. It provides them with scenarios for learning to compromise, and discovering the benefits of cooperating. A lesson in teamwork. They discover that their voice matters and that their opinion has value. Let the children participate in decision-making whenever it is practically possible.

Q: What should I do if my child does not want to cooperate with the other children and denies participating in a play?

A: You could ask, "Are you feeling anxious about performing in the play? Are you in anxiety?" Because that is a feeling he may have. You can also ask him, "Are you afraid of making mistakes?" And follow up with the offering, "Would you like to talk about how you feel and what you really need?"

I would try to be emphatic with anything he says. Then he will likely discover what unfulfilled need is behind his strategy of not participating in the play. It may come from his need for protection or some other need. Knowing the need, he will may decide to participate in the play as he now understands how to fulfill that need by being part of a group.

Whether he decides to participate or not, he knows that you love him and are ready to hear him and accept him for whatever choice he makes. He'll be relieved to know that there is no pressure on him to take part in the play.

Please don't lay a guilt trip on him, "You know how hard it was to make time for coming here, and how expensive all that gas was! And now you do not want to be in the play! What kind of child *are* you? *I'm* your mother! You *will* participate in that play today! And you *will* like it, and I will be proud of you, whether you like it or not, and you *will* have fun, whether you like it or not!" That is not the way to convince a child or anyone.

How to Comfort a Child

Q: What should the parents do if the child does not want to stop crying and screaming?

A: Please don't tell them to shut up, it usually doesn't work. They will usually scream more. Often, when I am in an airplane, one of the children on the plane will be crying and his mother will say, "Shut up, you are bothering everybody!" Sometimes they're sitting right next to me! I put my earplugs on! The other passengers are looking at him like he's a demon. They think I'm the parent since I am sitting next to him. So, the passengers think I'm a demon, too!

Put the relationship first. Be empathic with the child and cool-headed enough to comprehend what they are trying to communicate. When children do something, they are trying to communicate something specific.

There are two interesting videos made by the person who wrote the books titled *The Happiest Baby on the Block* and *The Happiest Toddler on the Block*. In these books the author, explains how children's activities are attempts to communicate something. A toddler is a two year old. The child is expressing a need for something, and if you reflect that need back it will cool him or her down. The parent says, "You are crying. You have a need for food." Or "You are so tired. You really have a need for sleep." Sometimes the parent might even say, "... (yawn) I really want to sleep," taking the child's position. I suggest those books to those with really young children.

The most effective thing one can do is to be receptive and responsive to communication. Start looking at it like this: 'Crying is *communication*. No child ever cries just to make me miserable.'

Q: *What if the child should go to bed but he starts asking for a pen and paper, and if he cannot get it just cries?*

A: What is wrong with giving a child a pen and paper? There's nothing wrong with a request, unless it is a request ask for liquor or something harmful. You don't give a child anything they want, but what harm can something like a pen and a piece of paper do? Besides, being a little cranky or demanding is also a symptom of being tired. When people – even little children – are very tired they'll begin feeling insecure. Your child is actually asking you, "Do you love me? I need you to show me, because I'm not sure right now." By being demanding and by crying they are looking for love and affection. Really what the child needs at that point is visible assurance of love and affection. Asking for pen and paper that late in the evening is simply a strategy for fulfilling the need for love. That is all.

It is harder for the child to cry than to just ask you, "Mommy, do you really love me? I need to know." They are crying because they are in distress. Crying is not a pleasant experience for a child. If they think that they can get the need met by simply asking, "Daddy can I have a pen and some paper?" they would prefer doing that over crying anytime. It's not a pen and paper that they are asking for, it is something else; something that is a whole lot more important to the child, *your* love. Please start recognizing that they are not crying for a pen and some paper. There is an *underlying* need. If they are using the strategy of crying much of the time, it is may be because they feel *insecure*. You have to guess the need. Look for the underlying need behind the strategy.

Once you understand what the underlying need is, you can come up with the right strategy for helping the child fulfill that need. If you let yourself be snowed under by the child's external strategy you will probably not be successful in attempting to change the undesirable behavior.

When adults are tired, we sometimes get a little cranky too, and insecure and even depressed. We have those symptoms when we're over-exhausted, so what to speak of a kid who is not yet developed enough to identify where his feelings come from. We tend to project our own situation onto others. We'll assume that a child is doing things (like asking for pen and paper) for the same reason we would if we were in that same position. A child has limited abilities to understand things.

We may superimpose a high philosophical understanding that took us twenty-five years to attain on a ten-year old kid. Then we get upset if they don't understand that they are not the body. How unfair is that? The kid simply doesn't have the means for understanding all those high philosophical truths.

Sometimes you'll see a kid go through gurukula, come out at age 21, and not even comprehend the ABCs of Krishna conscious philosophy, even though they can quote so many slokas by heart. I run into that all the time. All these years in gurukula, good teachers, good philosophy, and they do not know yet that they are not their body. So, be a little compassionate with your demanding crying child who doesn't yet have the skills to find a logic-based strategy.

Q: What do you mean by saying that they do not know?

A: Not even theoretically – because the philosophy was taught to them in the same way that you learnt history, "Columbus crossed the ocean blue in fourteen-hundred ninety-two." But I do not visualize Columbus crossing the ocean blue in fourteen-hundred ninety-two. It is just a fact that I was taught. I don't even understand what it means, but I know that the queen sent him on the Santa Maria.

You learned all kinds of facts in school, and most of them were not really relevant to you, because you were young. I studied history, and I hated history in school. I didn't see any connection with real life. Now I love history. If someone talks to me about World War II, where this or that general was, and when, and what he did there, I really like it. I mean I *like* it. What can I say? I like Krishna, too! He is kinda nice. But it's totally amazing that I like world history when I absolutely hated it as a kid. You see, with my brain being so young at that time, I just couldn't understand the psychological, sociological, and political dynamics that made it interesting. It was a rotten bunch of stupid facts then. Now it's different for me because my level of understanding is more advanced. We don't understand that about a child. We think they're just a small adult that does things for the same reasons as we do. But that isn't true.

Q: What should I do when my child asks for a cookie before the meal?

A: Whatever they need, take the time to sit down and talk. Don't just hand over the cookie. Sit down and talk. Talk about the needs you both have. Somewhere in the discussion you'll suggest different, healthier strategies. "Would you be willing to take the cookie after the meal?" Start to talk about his or her needs. That will open up the possibility for talking about different strategies to fulfill those needs, as in 'there's more than one way.' Then you allow them to decide what way meets the specific need best. "Yes, alright, here's the cookie for you, but really, the best time to take the cookie – based on our considerations of your health that we discussed – would be don't you think?"

Usually we expect him or her to accept something, without explaining the reason for it. That's like buying a smart phone without asking for the owner's manual. How intelligent is that? Many times, we do not even consider giving the child a chance to *ask* for an explanation.

If you favor cooperation over coercion, then it's best for you to think about a logical reason behind actions, ahead of time. The child will appreciate the effort you make to explain things in terms of *your* needs and *his* or *her* needs. "I have a need for you to be healthy. It is really important to me. Look, I don't have any teeth left, because I always ate cookies before dinner when I was young. So now my teeth are like stars – they come out at night." By taking the time to dialogue with the child, you will more likely be able to understand whether they are really hungry or not. The child could be really hungry even if it isn't dinner time yet. In that case, they might be allowed to eat before dinnertime. Try not to impose artificial eating regulations on your child. "You have to sit down now. It is dinnertime. You have to eat everything on your plate."

My mother used to tell me, "You have to eat everything on your plate." I said, "No." And sometimes the meal ended up on my head. I remember one time there was soup, hot soup, and I said, "I am not touching it." And

148

she said, "If you do not eat it, I will put it on your head." And I said, "I dare you to do that,"– and a bowl of piping hot soup ended up on my head.

The Results of Unskilled Empathic Parenting – and Some Advice

Q: Children do not see beyond their immediate needs. How can we explain to them their long term needs? And what if we do not have the needed time or expertise to do that?

A: It's very valuable and life-contributing to let children learn to see beyond their immediate needs by themselves. And it requires patience and facilitation on our part. We're dealing with children who don't want to get up the next morning, don't want to go to school, and don't want to sit down and chant.

My advice to anyone planning to have children is to expect dedicating the major portion of their life to caring for them. In the United States parents of the first generation of children raised in the Krsna consciousness movement often didn't put the necessary time into caring for them. As a result we have a large number of children from that first generation who do not want to have much to do with Krishna consciousness at this point, at least strict Krishna consciousness.

We held great expectations for them. Prabhupada called them Vaikuntha children. We thought they would grow up without interest in video games or any other non-Krishna conscious activities. In our minds we saw them become five- and six-year-old little Prahlada Maharajas, would learn the whole Bhagavad-gita by heart while we were out on sankirtan. We imagined coming back at night to find these pure devotees chanting sixty-four rounds a day.

Like that story of Raghunandan in Caitanya Bhagavata. He was the son of Mukunda. Mukunda, being a doctor, would go out to see patients. Once he told five-year old little Raghunandan, "Take care of the Deities and make sure that They eat!" Raghunandan offered food to the Deities, but he did not know the mantras. So, he started crying, and the Deities stepped off the altar and started to eat. When his father returned, he asked, "Where is the maha-prasadam?" Raghunandan said, "There is no maha-prasadam.

Krishna ate everything." His father did not believe him, but Raghunandan showed him how Krishna had eaten everything.

We thought all our children would be like that. What happened, instead, to this first generation of children was very disappointing. That was due to our lack of time, concern, and understanding of how to treat children. My advice to you is to plan spending most of your time on raising children, if you want to have any.

Q: Still, there could be circumstances when as a mother, I cannot give attention to the children because I have something more important to do. For example, guests come or we want to do some service. How we could handle such situations?

A: But what *is* the most important? The children! When I was young and my parents had guests over, I wasn't allowed to sit at the table with my parents. I had to sit at another table. I felt sad and thought I was being rejected. I still feel hurt because of that. "I want to be with you." "No, you have to sit there with the other kids." Talking about it even today practically brings tears to my eyes, because of what I had perceived as rejection. We should try to see how the children are perceiving things from their perspective. They are emotionally very vulnerable.

Q: So just put the child's needs above all?

A: For a mother, the child's needs always come first, the husband's second. That sometimes frustrates the husband. Before they were number one, and as soon as the child arrives, they get bumped. "Who are *you*? Oh, right, I do remember you now." Srila Prabhupada wrote to a pujari that her most important service now was to raise her child – one of the Vaikuntha children. She asked him about it, because she wanted to understand what was more important. "Your business is child worship now." The *shastras* see child service as more important than anything else, especially for the mother. Even Mother Yashoda loves Krishna more than Nanda Maharaja.

Q: While worshiping the Deities how can we follow the principles of cleanliness if we have young children?

A: You must not say to your child, "Do not touch me because I have to worship the Deities." In the child's perception, they were just rejected.

You have no idea how it can affect the child. "I'm not allowed to touch mommy because she is worshiping Krishna. Therefore Krishna must be my enemy." I have seen that happen with children. I advise householders not to keep *shilas*– but they don't listen. When you worship *shalagram shilas*, you cannot have any impurity in your home. Your first duty is to take care of the children. Have Gaura-Nitai deities instead. You can't be worrying about cleanliness standards when you have children. If you try this, the children will likely be turned off by Krishna consciousness, maybe forever. Avoid doing elaborate deity worship if you have young children. You don't want the children grabbing the Deities and chew on Them. They *will* do that. Put the Deities high enough, or, for the sake of the children, put them away for a while.

Your first duty is to serve the Vaishnavas, not the Deities. If you serve the Deities nicely but you do not serve the Vaishnavas, particularly a defenseless Vaishnava like a child, the Deity will not accept your service. That's what Lord Kapiladeva in the Bhagavatam calls "offering oblations to the ashes," in other words useless. Your first priority is to serve the devotees. In *Kali yuga*, deity worship is not a primary, but a secondary activity. Your family members are devotees. Your husband, wife, children, are all devotees. Serving them is most important. It necessitates a mindset change, a priority change. Don't run to the temple to first serve the Deities. Serve your family, Serve your children, and be compassionate and empathic with them. You only have one chance with the children. When they are older, it is too late.

Q: I have a child, a two-year-old daughter. We live in a town where there is no possibility for her to associate with other devotee children. Is it better for her to go to a kindergarten where the other children are not devotee children or should we have a nanny to take care of her at home?

A: That's your decision and has to be reached with the child's needs foremost in your mind. It is my experience that children will be inclined to accept the parents as role models if they perceive the parents to be in tune with their needs, feel unconditionally loved by them, and don't hear them argue. Then wherever they may be, with or without a nanny, going to school or not, they'll develop their own sense of morality and will be strong devotees. As Prabhupada said, example is more important than

151

precept. Your example of love, devotion and Krishna consciousness is more important than what you say.

Q: When I was little my parents banned me from playing video games. And the first time when I got money to buy a sandwich I did not buy a sandwich but I went to a video club to play video games. What to do with my children? Should I give them a minimum of video games or no video games at all?

A: First of all, I would say if you set a good example of being Krishna conscious yourself and loving towards them, the question will answer itself. Like my relationship with Prabhupada: he never told to me not to do this, not to do that; but because I see Prabhupada as my perfect role model I want to be like him, too. I do not want to *be* Prabhupada but I *do* want to be like him. I love him so much that there is no question of doing anything different. That is what we have to bring out, love. Then everything else will be taken care of.

CHAPTER FIVE

Gratitude and Appreciation

In authoritative-type cultures, individuals are largely motivated by rewards, praise, compliments, money, punishments, blame, shame, or guilt. In contrast, in an empathic culture, individuals are motivated by the desire to contribute to life by meeting their own needs and helping others meet their needs. Gratitude will naturally be expressed from the heart, as a celebration, not as a means for personal gain. At times, even money can be exchanged but not by demand, rather to show sincere gratitude. As taught throughout this book, gratitude is expressed with the same basic components of empathic communication. In other words, one shares the impact of a particular action with feelings and needs.

It's helpful to differentiate between self-focused gratitude (praise) and empathic gratitude in which we are authentic and clear about our intentions. The following are examples to help illustrate the difference as we continue to practice giving and receiving empathically.

1. Motivation/intent

- Empathic: Celebrating how someone has contributed to our life

- Self-focused: Offering with the intent to gain personally

2. Language

- **Empathic gratitude**:
  "When you did _____ I felt _____ because of my need (or value) for _____ ."

- **Self-focused gratitude**:
  "You are so good at doing _____ , it would be really nice if I had someone to do something like that for me."

Use these examples to practice, as well as to reflect on possible motives. If there is something personally motivating the gratitude or appreciation, think about ways to make it fully empathic, genuine. This will support the goal of being truly compassionate.

The Grace of Gratitude Past

Often in the past there have been instances that we wanted to share appreciation or gratitude, but didn't take the time. Think about a time you did not offer gratitude, and why.

Exercise

Take time to express gratitude to someone who contributed to your life in the past, but you did not have the opportunity to do it then. You can use pen and paper or offer it in your heart. This can be done for someone who is no longer present or alive. You can make a list of people you didn't offer gratitude to, and then work through the list making those offerings. Gratitude or appreciation doesn't necessarily have to be verbal.

Healthy Bragging

Another aspect of gratitude or appreciation is expressing our personal successes, as we can be joyful about having contributed positively through devotional service, and perhaps accomplishing something we didn't realize we were capable of doing. It's important to celebrate our successes. Although it's important, there is the need to be aware of the motive. What do you think would be sincere or effective 'bragging'?

Things to keep in mind:

> Don't use static (generalized) language by saying something like, "I am great!" Brag about what was done or actually happened.

> Be specific about what you did, how you feel now (not in the past), and what need was met.

> No sneaky bragging! This is "fishing" for a compliment and self-centered/motivated, as
> opposed to celebrating self-accomplishment or the joy of something done out of devotion.

> Try to check for your internal motive and make an adjustment according to the underlying feelings and needs that are stimulating the motive.

Here is an example: Yesterday I was able to cook for that sick devotee. I am really happy about that. It really met my need for contributing to another's well being.

How Can Gratitude Be Shown and Received?

Receiving and showing gratitude are our core needs. Expressing gratitude does not mean praising them. Real appreciation is accompanied by a celebratory mood. For example: "When you agreed to help me with the seminar I felt great joy in my heart because I have a need for truly supportive help. Thank you very much for doing this for me." We need appreciation (not praise). When you express gratitude you are contributing to a person's well being.

When gratitude is expressed, it's important to avoid displaying false humility instead of sharing the real emotion or feeling. Example: "Oh no, I'm just so fallen . I'm just a worm in stool. I am actually even lower than that" That is nothing but a dishonest pretense of humility. True humility is not evidenced by "thinking less of yourself, but by thinking of yourself less" often. Focus on being happy to serve Krishna and your spiritual master. The process involves being vulnerable and expressing your emotions openly.

Receiving gratitude is part of the process, and allows the other person to make an offering and fulfill their personal need as well. By receiving gratitude graciously rather than with guilt you are rendering service towards the person offering the gratitude. Refrain from saying, "I don't deserve it."

In review, our expression of gratitude encompasses observations, feelings. needs and possibly a request. When we respond to gratitude we have received, we'll move through that same process of observation, feelings and needs with a possible request.

Examples of Sharing & Receiving Gratitude

"My dear Srila Prabhupada, when you accepted me as your disciple in 1972, I felt great joy and relief in my heart, because I have a need for purpose in life, and for understanding how to help people in practical ways without prolonging their suffering in this material world. I have a need to know how to express and receive love. I also have a need to know about the meaning of life, the purpose of life and the nature of God. I want to thank you very much, Srila Prabhupada, and please keep me always under the shelter of your lotus feet. Jaya Srila Prabhupada!"

Here you see a specific observation expressed, a feeling expressed, a need expressed, and a request made. Go through my expression of gratitude to Prabhupada and find each of these elements.

Conversation with Vrajalila devi dasi: "Dear Bir Krishna Maharaja, when I heard you in the camp sharing the technology of empathic communication I felt joyful. I felt relieved. I felt blissful. I felt peaceful. I felt like I belong, because I have such a need to belong, I have such a need to understand how empathic communication can be transmitted to the devotees. I have a need to learn more about compassion. I have a need to learn more about caring. I have a need to give compassion, to give care. I have a need to honor my spiritual master. Maharaja, you have fulfilled those needs."

Response to Vrajalila's gratitude: "Yesterday when I was talking to you about this seminar, you said to me: 'I'm so happy that you are teaching this in ISKCON.' And then I asked you the question do you think Bhakti Tirtha Maharaja would be happy with this? And you said 'yes.' I really have a need to connect and to be serving my dear friends in Krishna consciousness, and to associate with them eternally. So, thank you very much!"

Expressing gratitude can be difficult because it requires being open, being vulnerable. It does not matter whether you are showing gratitude to one person or to many, you simply follow this same process. When you allow yourself to be vulnerable, people are able to appreciate and love you more. You are giving them permission, the opportunity, to do the same.

This heartfelt communication is very useful for resolving problems with other people, because you can give your ear to someone's feelings and needs without making any judgments or demands.

CHAPTER SIX

From Power to Personal

If You Go To Lanka You Will Become Ravana

"This afternoon, Prabhupada sat at his desk, his managers before him. He lamented that it has been his constant headache ever since the temple was opened a year and half ago, that no person can be found who can manage it nicely. With a wry humor born from the barren seeds of repeated, unavailing attempts to find a competent manager, he smiled and quoted an old saying: *yaya sei lanka sei haya ravana*, "Anyone who comes to Lanka, he becomes a Ravana.""

As Lord Acton stated, "Power tends to corrupt and absolute power corrupts absolutely." And so in institutions where power lies in the hands of a few or a single individual, we can perceive that corruption and abuse of power are concomitant factors. There are myriad reasons for this, but the end result is that those in power tend to view those to whom they have authority over as objects rather than subjects. This occurs in religious institutions, in the armed forces, in the government, in prisons and many other places. Sociologists have studied this phenomenon in depth.

An example of the effect of power is Henry Ford. In the beginning of the Ford Motor Company, Mr. Ford treated his workers compassionately as if they were his dear children. There are instances where he doubled their salaries as an expression of love for them. When the Ford Motor Company grew more and more, his treatment of them began to resemble that of a tyrant.

In the famous Stanford 'prison experiment' done by Professor Zimbardo, the students who were assigned power positions and were acting as jailors, became so abusive to the students who were acting as prisoners that the experiment had to be terminated sooner than had been planned to prevent the prisoner-students from suffering permanent emotional and physical harm. Surprisingly, even Professor Zimbardo who was supervising the study allowed the abuse to go on.

Studies show that when one gets power one sees people as objects for fulfilling ones' strategies, rather than as persons. They use the authoritarian-type behaviors of diagnosis, demand, deserve, and denial that cut off communication and empathy. "I did it because I had to. They were misbehaving and had to be corrected. Anyway it was my job, and I was just following orders." Utilizing the tools of EC (Empathic Communication) it is possible to see that these blocks of communication that we have previously described tend to affect the consciousness of persons in power. That is to say, they:

1. **Diagnose** those under them; i.e. see them as employees, prisoners, bhaktas, etc. (labels) and not as dynamic, sentient entities.

2. Because of that, they **demand** obedience from them.

3. When those under them don't do what the authority demands, they get angry and blame the person for their anger (**denial**), then think the disobedient persons **deserve** to be punished or suffer under the hands of God (or His representative).

In religious societies, this problem is particularly prominent due to the inherent diagnostic tendency in religions. Religious literatures are rife with diagnoses of persons who are either strict adherents of the prescribed path or deviants from that path. Once a label is applied, dealings with that person tend to be in terms of that label. Hence shades of grey in these interactions give way to black and white judgments. This tendency can even be observed between peers and leads to such rough dealings that many people become discouraged on their spiritual path.

Here are some actions I recommend as being helpful to prevent the above behavior:

1. Constant introspection by those on the spiritual path

2. Take the perspective of the person being judged

3. Establish ombudsman systems in spiritual organizations

4. Institute team-building exercises that include all levels of the organization

Hierarchy does have a place in society because it helps to keep society regulated. We should however, take up the motto of "Power With" rather than "Power Over."

How Does Varnashram Fit In?

In a Varnashram society people are engaged according to their psycho-physical nature. This means the type of work they do is determined by the combination of the modes which affect their subtle and gross bodies. These same modal ingredients also affect their living situation.

We understand this is external and relates to our material nature, which is temporary; and our eternal spiritual nature usually has no relationship to our present material condition.

However, while one is in this world, it is important to act externally according to one's temporary nature and engage that temporary nature in Krishna's service. Even if one is completely spiritually conscious the necessity is there to set an example for those who are not. This teaching is brought out in the Gita in which Arjuna is taught these two points: you should act according to your nature, and you should act in such a way as to set an example for others. Even Krishna mentions this point in relationship to Himself.

yad yad acarati sresthas
tat tad evetaro janah
say at pramanam kurute
lokas tad anuvartate

"Whatever action a great man performs, common men follow. And whatever standards he sets by exemplary acts, all the world pursues."33

Varnashram is the means for dealing with ones' gross and subtle needs in an appropriate *dharmic* fashion. Everyone has basic needs, as we have described earlier in the book. However, strategies for fulfilling these needs differ in accordance with ones' psychophysical nature.

Everyone has the need for love for example. In the completely Krishna conscious state, that need is fulfilled in relationship to Radha and Krishna

---

33 *Bhagavad-gita, 3.21*

and Vaiṣṇava Seva. In the conditioned state, one in the grhasta ashram fulfills this need by marriage, developing love for Krishna, and loving exchanges with guru the Vaishnavas. In the brahmacari, vanaprastha and sannyasa stages the appropriate means are to immerse oneself in Krishna consciousness, and to engage in the six loving exchanges with the guru, and other Vaishnavas. The same needs are there, but the strategies are different.

The same principle also applies to one's work. Therefore, it is best to work in such a way that the mind is absorbed in Krishna's service. For some, that may mean preaching and studying. For others, it may mean managing. For others, it may mean making money for Krishna. And for others, it may mean manual work.

It is helpful to have senior guides who, understanding one's individual's nature, facilitate one in developing the appropriate strategies for addressing one's needs. This allows for an exchange that is both respectful and cooperative, and focuses on strategies that are supportive of the ultimate goal of pure love of God.

All You Need Is Love

Oftentimes the word 'love' is seen in a negative way by aspiring spiritualists. We usually associate the word 'love' with mundane romantic affairs. Mundane romance doesn't help one advance towards the goal of realizing oneself to be a pure spiritual entity, dedicated to the service of the Lord.

We use the expression 'pure love' to indicate the state of desiring to please the Lord without any subtle or gross motivation. Srila Rupa Goswami elaborates on this concept of pure love in the nutshell verse from the *Bhakti Rasamrita Sindhu:* "*When first-class devotional service develops, one must be devoid of all material desires, knowledge obtained by monistic philosophy, and fruitive action. The devotee must constantly serve Krsna favorably, as Krsna desires.*"

I would like to present a third understanding of love in the context of relationships between devotees of the Lord. This meaning is indicated in Rupa Goswami's *Upadeshamrita* (verse 4): "*Offering gifts in charity, accepting charitable gifts, revealing one's mind in confidence, inquiring confidentially, accepting prasadam and offering prasadam are the six symptoms of love shared by one devotee and another.*" It is quite interesting that Srila Prabhupada uses the word 'symptoms' in the translation. These are external symptoms of affectionate dealings, but what is occurring in the heart is most important, otherwise it may be a hypocritical show. One should be interacting with the devotees with the desire to please them. *This* is love.

It is easy to understand the spiritual need for loving others, being loved and loving oneself. Srila Rupa Goswami in the above verse from the *Upadesamrta* makes this abundantly clear and Srila Prabhupada states in his purport to this verse: *"The life of the Krsna conscious society is nourished by these six types of loving exchange among the members."* We understand that when we love the devotees, Krishna becomes pleased with us. In fact, He is more pleased by our service to His devotees than He is by direct service to Him. A devotee is also described:

> *"A Vaisnava is so liberal that he is prepared to risk everything to rescue the conditioned souls from material existence. Srila*

Vasudeva Datta Thakura is universal love itself, for he was willing to sacrifice everything and fully engage in the service of the Supreme Lord." 34

"As such, if we concentrate our loving propensities upon Krsna only, then immediately universal love, unity and tranquility will be automatically realized."35

"...but our actual identity should be, "I am Krsnas." *When we think in this way, we are thinking in Krsna consciousness. Only in this way can universal love among all living entities be established."36*

"But a devotee, a pure lover of God, he loves everyone. Just like we are. "37

Love is an extremely important need for devotees, not only from the emotional standpoint, but also from the mental, physical and spiritual standpoint. As far as the physical realm is concerned there is quite a bit of evidence that the need for love is connected with our well-being. When the opposite of love (hate) is experienced, one's health can be adversely affected even to the point of being subject to life-threatening diseases such as cancer. Some of the diseases we are experiencing may be due to an unfulfilled need for loving exchanges. There is quite a bit of scientific evidence for this. Here are several studies which validate this point.

The Harvard Study

There was a study done at Harvard that illustrated the connection between health and the need for love. In 1950, 126 men were chosen and asked about the closeness of their relationships with their parents. The follow up was done 35 years later. According to the medical records of the participants, 91 percent of the participants who stated that they did not

---

34 *Caitanya Caritamrta Madhya, 15.163*

35 *Krishna Book, Preface*

36 *Krishna Consciousness, The Matchless Gift, Chapter 3 – Learning to Love*

37 *Bhagavad-gita 3.27 Class, by Srila Prabhupada – Melbourne, June 27, 1974*

have a warm relationship with their mothers had serious chronic diseases like heart disease, high blood pressure, ulcers and alcoholism. Amongst those who had a warm relationship with their mothers only 45 percent had these types of diseases. In addition, 100 percent of those who rated their relationships with both their mothers and fathers low in warmth had the aforementioned types of diseases, whereas only 47 percent of those who rated their relationships with their mothers and fathers highly had these illnesses.

In another Harvard study, it was concluded that the best predictor of who would get cancer later on in life was based on the nature of the father-son relationships in childhood and youth.

The Roseto Study

In a study done in Roseto, Pennsylvania the need for loving relationships was further illustrated. People who lived in Roseto had a very low mortality rate from heart attacks when compared to neighboring towns, even though the normal risk factors considered (smoking, diet, pollution) were the same. The cause of this was traced to the fact that the majority of the residents in Roseto were from the same town in Italy and had maintained very close community and familial relationships. This all changed in the 1960s and 70s when the next generation became less cohesive, fragmented, and people were more isolated. Then their mortality rate rose to the same level as the neighboring towns.

The Alameda County Study

In 1965 almost 7,000 men and women were studied in this county near San Francisco. In the ensuing years, it was shown that those who lacked social and community ties were 1.9 (190 %) to 3.1 (310%) times more likely to die during the nine-year follow up.

The Tecumseh Study

It was shown that when social relationships were broken or decreased, disease rates increased 200-300 percent in a 10-12-year period.

The Swedish Study

17,000 men and women between the ages of twenty-nine to seventy-four were studied. It was concluded that those who were the most lonely and isolated were four times more likely to die prematurely during a six-year period.

The Finnish Study

In Finland, a similar study of more than 13,000 people showed that over a 5-9 year period, men who were socially isolated had a 2-3 times increased rate of death. That's 200-300 percent increase!

A Rabbit Study

Even amongst animals, the need for love is connected with health. In one study, rabbits were given a diet to increase the incidence of heart disease. The rabbits that were regularly handled had 60 percent less plaque on their arteries!

There are many more studies. The evidence is clear. In addition to being spiritually necessary, loving exchanges are required to maintain our health and our ability to function as instruments for the Supreme Lord. I was often surprised when my dear God brother Bhakti Tirtha Maharaj would sign his letters, "with love." Now I can understand what he was teaching us by using this closing. In successful religious institutions, we find the members are quite physical in expressing their affection for each other. For example, after the Sunday services at a church the congregation generally goes around shaking each others' hands or demonstrating their affection in different ways. We can learn from these empathic interactions.

Conclusion

I have written this brief introduction to Empathic Communication with the hope that I can contribute to the lives of all the readers. My desire is to serve the Vaisnavas according to my capacity, and by so doing gain the blessings of my spiritual master, His Divine Grace A.C. Bhaktivedanta Swami Prabhupada. If I have his blessings, my life is successful.

Krishna loves all of us equally. Srila Prabhupada stated in a lecture that Krishna is meditating on how to protect and maintain us. He loves us so much that this love causes Him anxiety. We should be willing to take on some of that anxiety as Srila Prabhupada has done for us.

TESTIMONIALS

Devotees participating in an empathic communication seminar express their appreciations.

"I learned a lot about myself and I learned how to be more sensitive towards others. [What] helped me the most was the unity of the group. There is hope for improvement. SO GOOD TO HAVE PEOPLE LIKE YOU IN ISKCON!!! Very glad and happy to get to know Maharaj BIR KRISHNA GOSWAMI especially that he has found a suitable way to get to the root of the problem and a solution to help devotees to become HAPPY! A DEEP THANK YOU!"

"The workshop was helpful in regard to better relationships. The dance flow I think we could go even deeper. I felt more and more comfortable and happy. The issues were appealing to me, although I would have loved to have more about close relationships. The trainer was very humorous and honest and able to give everything needful to learn the lessons."

"I understood what it means NVC. Most helpful was to see examples, to do exercises, and later reflection. It helped me to think about how to communicate my feelings and needs. 90% I was satisfied with answers. When we were doing the exercises, I was happy to see how to use tools. Very comfortable, therefore it could be longer. All issues were interesting to me. I would like to deal especially with the child care, relationships, mediation."

"Although I could participate just for one day, I got curious to find out more about it – and I am sure the whole seminar would even enrich my life much more than it did in one day. The only frustrating thing was the date – a normal working day, so I could just attend one day. Maybe next time a weekend? Everything was perfect, everybody felt fine and like in a family. I will use whatever I managed to learn here in my daily life."

"Joyful, thankful and hopeful to get an improvement of our community Goloka Dhama."

"There was no negative feedback. Actually, I have yet no idea of how helpful it was, because I must put at least some of the items/strategies into practice."

"Yes, practical examples opened to see things from different angle to invite outside people. I was satisfied to be with the devotees, I got answered questions on how to control angry children. Focus on needs helped me to relate to the person. Frustrating was fast speed, long sessions. Workshop opened my eyes for coming out of the box, positive approach on negativity, to appreciate more others and one self. I would like more opening of the windows, more fresh air, more husband/wife topics."

"EC workshop (Dance flow) transformed the feelings and showed the needs, quotes of Srila Prabhupada (BG, SB), volunteers to guide me through the dance flow, seeing others how they were present, practical appliance, one to one exercise, really enriched my life. I felt very connected and grounded. Connected to me and my need, I can listen to others. I would like to have a whole week of training."

"When I attended your seminar on empathic communication in Croatia this year I was very positively surprised for two reasons: The first one is that I had expected that the seminar would be similar to the ones on empathic listening skills that I had already attended some years ago by somebody else but then I found out that the techniques you were teaching us are completely different and even more effective and practical than anything else that I had learned previously. The other reason is that I felt very much relieved to see that there are senior Vaishnavas in Srila Prabhupada's movement who are caring so much for the real needs of devotees, especially the need for open and honest communication between leaders and their subordinates. This was often missing in the past. Your seminar gave me some new hope and confidence for my spiritual life. I returned from Croatia with a new positive vision and the inner certainty that my real needs are properly taken care of by senior Vaishnavas. I want to express my heartfelt gratitude towards you for this experience by supporting your training in our local yatra."

I attended your seminar in Croatia this summer that you gave …. I liked it very much and I felt very enlivened, enlightened and rich inside because I have a need to learn and understand phenomena around me in Krsna consciousness and in the world. You fulfilled my need so it made me so grateful and indebted to you."

"Your presentation at the camp was a big inspiration for me and left some transformation in my heart."

"It's hard to be specific about the points you made, the actions you did, because during those three weeks you give me so much knowledge and realizations throughout lectures and your presentations. It is completely different when I listen to you live. How to say, it really gets me, touches me deeply. Can not define all the feelings but, for example, your body language with sense of humor inspires, aliveness and motivates to joyfully serve and be happy while trying to reach KCON. I need to admit, the more I listen to EC and learning, I'm realizing how important that is. Through EC we are self realizing ourselves in very practical way and have a chance to really understand others, also to connect to them. This realization gives me a great hope to be compassionate towards everybody one day, it's a reachable goal in life, yeeeeh I can see it now, it's so amazing, it gives me a vision. And my friend said, who doesn't have a vision – watch television! Thank you so much for helping me to open my eyes inside. I am so grateful and thankful that you are my spiritual master and I honestly want to help you in your mission."

"First of all, I want to thank you very much for your really wonderful course on "Empathic Communication." I liked it so much and think that applying these things which we learned will change a lot in dealings with others. When I listened during the course, I felt, that these things are so logical and it would be almost common sense to deal and communicate like this (and, the truth is always so simple), but it made such a difference, that you expressed all this in words and presented it so systematically and analytically. The distinctions between feelings and needs and the fact that feelings are only connected to needs is so important to know, because one will be able to better understand oneself and others and on this basis deal much nicer with others. I guess it will also help to not become a helpless victim of one's emotions but to understand...There would be many more things to say, I just wanted to express shortly my gratitude and only mentioned a little of what really touched me. Thank you so much."

"After coming home from this l, I have seen that my life has improved on different levels. Thanks to your seminar, I start to become more thoughtful. Now, when I see somebody speaking or acting with anger or dissatisfaction, I don't try to see the anartha behind the speech, but rather I try to see what the unfulfilled need behind the person's words or behavior. It is a revolutionary way of perceiving things.

This experience is so nice and pleasing to the heart. I tried to apply it in the camp already in the few situations, and it worked. Now, I am in the deep introspection days, to see what my unfulfilled needs are, and how to organize my life better. Then, I have a conviction that I will be able also to help others to do the same. I am feeling very happy, encouraged and enthusiastic to continue with my devotional service after this seminar. Why? Specifically, because you have convinced me through the seminar that the needs are not bad and that they are natural. Second, as I already wrote, but I want to thank you for that gift once again, through the seminar I have accepted the new perspective of myself and the others when we are dissatisfied, angry or frustrated. I don't look now at myself or others as a low class fallen souls, filled with lust, anger and greed, but rather that we are all individual personalities who are missing something in our lives in order to be happy, peaceful and satisfied. Therefore, acting and speaking harshly. Somehow, I have impression that we are the entities of love, and that our basic need is to love, be loved and to have deep loving exchanges with each other. Thanks to the seminar, I was able also to get more in touch with [someone] who I respect very much. But now, I get a beautiful chance to see him in different role than usually. He helped me to understand how to be specific and what does it really mean. From then on, I became aware how impersonal I am, sometimes. But now, this word "SPECIFIC" by your mercy, helped me to understand better what real personalism really is.

As you said, when somebody come to you and ask you for the blessings, you just said: "Ok, blessings!" Now, I perceive it differently. One of my devotee friends told me that Srila Prabhupada said that: "Taking care of the details is the symptom of love." Through the seminar, I went through different phases. At first, I was completely hopeless that I would be able to understand anything. I have analyzed what made me feel like that. It's because many time I failed in my attempts to understand properly myself and others. That impression was so strong and even nourished when I saw on the beginning of the seminar that I am mixing thoughts and feelings. Then, something changed, I don't remember at the moment what it was, but some "click" happen. Yes, maybe it was on Srila Bhaktivinode Thakur disappearance day, when it came to my mind that he also wrote how we have to keep the proper balance between the four needs. Inspiration increased when I get the realization:

"O, it seems that Bir Krishna Maharaja is trying to help us how to see our needs clearly, and what to do with them when we recognize them!" At that point I become very eager to learn more and to go deeper in the subject matter; although I have noticed that I don't understand something, even rebelling sometimes. By later on, during the seminar, all the doubts and rebellious thoughts were removed! At the end, I was so inspired with the seminar, that I felt a great pain for not being able to come to Croatian summer camp to go further and learn more how to apply it. I was in that state of mind for the few days; until I spoke with prabhu by phone. Then he told me that you will continue with the seminar on our camp next year. That information gave me such a great relief and such a great happiness, that I was almost jumping and dancing at my home. Dear Bir Krishna Maharaja, this was a story how one soul become transformed in sadhu sanga during your seminar. I was trying to describe what the phases I went through seminar and what was the final result, the deep conviction that we get on the Seminar something so precious that can change our lives tremendously. So, it was the letter from the heart (hopefully!). Now, I must "switch on" the brain and to apologize if my letter was not in accordance with the Vaiṣṇave etiquette."

"Learning EC has been a great help to my service to Prabhupada. Using EC principles allows me to feel energized when dealing with difficult problems, instead of exhausted. This effect holds true even if the problems cannot be solved. EC principles allow me to be a facilitator for others to find their own solutions to their problems. EC methods give a template for daily application of some of the basic ideology of Krishna consciousness. Understanding and using EC makes it much easier to feel compassion and to connect with others in a deep and meaningful way. It's a simple system to understand and apply, with much benefit. Sometimes the effects of using it seem nothing short of miraculous. I remain grateful to the devotees such as Bir Krishna Goswami who taught some EC seminars that I attended."

Works Cited

Rosenberg, Marshall B. *Nonviolent Communication: a Language of Life.*
Encinitas, CA: PuddleDancer Press, September 2003.

Rosenberg, Marshall B. *Raising Children Compassionately: Parenting the Nonviolent Communication Way.*
Encinitas, CA: PuddleDancer Press, 2005.

Rosenberg, Marshall B. *The Heart of Social Change: How to Make a Difference in Your World.*
Encinitas, CA: PuddleDancer Press, 2003.

Prabhupada, A. C. Bhaktivedanta Swami. *Bhagavad-gita as it is.*
Los Angeles, CA: Bhaktivedanta Book Trust, 1972.

Prabhupada, A. C. Bhaktivedanta Swami. *Srimad Bhagavatam.*
Los Angeles, CA: Bhaktivedanta Book Trust, 1980.

Prabhupada, A. C. Bhaktivedanta Swami. *Nectar of Devotion.*
Los Angeles, CA: Bhaktivedanta Book Trust, 1970.

Prabhupada, A. C. Bhaktivedanta Swami. *Nectar of Instruction.*
Los Angeles, CA: Bhaktivedanta Book Trust, 1975.

Prabhupada, A. C. Bhaktivedanta Swami. *Sri Caitanya Caritamrta.*
Los Angeles, CA: Bhaktivedanta Book Trust, 1975.

Thakura, Bhaktivinode. *Sri Caitanya-sikshamrita,* 1886

Printed in Great Britain
by Amazon

85364075R00106